ON BEING FATHER

FRANK FERRARA

ON BEING FATHER

*A Divorced Man
Talks About Sharing
the New Responsibilities
of Parenthood*

A DOLPHIN BOOK
DOUBLEDAY & COMPANY, INC.
GARDEN CITY, NEW YORK

1985

Library of Congress Cataloging in Publication Data

Ferrara, Frank.
On being father.

1. Single parents. 2. Divorced fathers.
3. Parenting. I. Title.
HQ759.915.F47 1985   306.8'56
ISBN 0-385-19128-6

Library of Congress Catalog Card Number 84–4068

First Edition

In memory of Gramps,
model of a sensitive and complete man.
He continues with me in spirit.

CONTENTS

INTRODUCTION

How Good a Single Father Are You?

This book is for the separated or divorced father who is having trouble keeping his ship afloat.

He's the captain of the ship—his own ship of life. Up to now, he's been sailing in pretty smooth waters—perhaps with a rocky passage to navigate now and then or an occasional storm or two to ride out, but nothing that he couldn't handle. But now that he and his wife have finally decided to call it quits, he finds that his ship has sailed right into the middle of a hurricane.

Before his separation, during the good days of his marriage, he had his hand firmly on the helm. The ship was steering her course, all the crew was accounted for, everything was shipshape. Now, after the separation, the helm is losing its power, the rudder is sticking, and the crew is jumping overboard. Not only that, but he's in hostile waters, having to dodge enemy torpedoes coming at him from every direction in the form of . . . fights with his ex-wife . . . legal tangles . . . money problems . . . contested divorce settlements . . . unfair custody arrangements . . . crippling lawyers' fees . . . and assorted emotional upheavals of all kinds.

The trouble with modern divorce is that along with losing your wife, you usually find yourself losing a lot of other things as well—your children, your money, your sanity, your self-respect, your peace of mind.

Practically every divorce has this double (or triple) whammy. You start off just wanting to be rid of your wife (or your wife wanting to be rid of you). Somewhere along the way, the situation snowballs, and before you know it, you're being stripped of all these other things you damn well *don't* want to be rid of.

The basic problem is that divorce is so much more than a mere legal matter. We may go into it thinking it's just a legal matter, but we soon learn different. It would be better if it were just a legal matter, but it inevitably seems to get tangled with a lot of other issues like money, children, emotions, and the like.

I know. I can speak from experience. After my wife and I separated, I went through a whole series of personal upsets and entanglements. I knew I didn't want to live with my wife anymore, but I didn't seem to be able to live without her. I was on my own for the first time in my life; I was lonely; I missed having a family around me. I had to go through all the emotions I've since learned every separated man goes through: guilt, anger, loneliness, despair, a sense of failure, insecurity, feelings of powerlessness and unfairness. My emotions were on a roller coaster. One day I'd be on top of the world with exhilaration at finally being free of all the marital obligations and expectations. The next day I'd be crying in my bed, unable to get up and face the day.

I got through it all eventually, but it took a long time—years, in fact. I learned a lot of things along the way—usually through bitter experience—and picked up a lot of advice—usually too late to do me any good. I wish I'd known all these things at the beginning. They'd have helped me get through my separation with a lot less trouble and grief. At the time, I didn't know where to turn for help and advice. Much of the time I didn't even know I *needed* help and advice.

I've since heard this same problem from hundreds of separated men. You might call it the IF-ONLY-I'D-KNOWN syndrome.

- "If only I'd known what to expect."
- "If only I'd known I wasn't the only one this was happening to."
- "If only I'd known where to meet other men in the same boat."

- "If only I'd known where to find advice and support."
- "If only I'd known how to deal more sanely with my wife."
- "If only I'd known how to take care of my kids."

That's what this book aims to be: a roundup of everything I (and all the other single fathers I've talked to over the years) have learned regarding how to cope with being a separated father. It's everything I wish someone had told *me* when I first got separated.

This book is for divorced *fathers*, not just divorced *men*. There's a big difference between the two. So many males, after their divorce, gradually cease being real fathers and simply become divorced men. They gradually drift away from their children and cease playing an effective fathering role in their children's lives. The children are usually living with the mother, and the father's physical separation all too often grows into a kind of emotional separation as well.

Not that men want to drift away from their kids. They don't. In fact, they're often desperate not to fade out of their children's lives. I know. After my own separation, I'd have gone crazy if I'd been separated from my son Christopher (I'd have had to go into heavy therapy, or I'd have tried to kidnap him, or . . . who knows what?). He meant too much to me for me to be able even to consider the possibility of losing him.

I was lucky: I got joint custody. My son is with me half the time, with his mother the other half. Most separated fathers aren't so lucky. The children go with the mother. That's the American Way of Divorce. The mother gets the children and the father gets "visitation rights." Faced by this vote of no confidence, the father finds himself drifting into a sort of limbo in which, without knowing exactly how it's happening, he sees his role as father evaporating until it's only a shadow of what it used to be.

He sees his children only once a week, or on weekends, and he finds himself becoming not a father but a kind of glorified social director—entertaining them, cooking for them, shopping for them—while they sit glued in front of the TV. After a while, his old relationship with his children is completely eroded and he's no longer a vital force in their lives.

It doesn't have to be this way.

It's not a foregone conclusion that a man has to lose his fatherly relationship with his children, his vital role in their lives. Even if his wife has custody, he can still remain their father. I've dealt with enough single fathers to know—to have *seen*—that it's possible to keep in vital touch with the children—if only you know how.

That's the problem, of course. Too many men just don't know how. They're flying blind. They haven't learned how to handle the situation in productive, effective ways. But if you do know how—and you can learn in this book—then you never have to fear that you'll become a stranger to your children.

Even when the man is lucky enough to get what he considers a fair custody arrangement (this is happening more and more every year), he's not over the hump yet. He's still faced with a big problem. He's won the right to his children. Now he's got to live with them. They're going to be with him, with *him alone,* for two weeks a month, or six months a year, or all summer, or whatever other arrangement he's agreed to. This isn't the easiest thing in the world to adjust to. He doesn't have his wife to lean on anymore. He's got to do all the work himself.

Frankly, most formerly married men are pretty poorly equipped to be single men again, much less single fathers. They've gotten used to having a wife around—that convenient person who seems to know all about children, knows all the things he hasn't bothered about: how to deal with them on a day-to-day basis, how to care for their illnesses, how to answer their questions, how to be patient with them, how to listen to them.

Now she's gone, and he, the man, finds that somehow he's got to develop all these new qualities, such as patience, forbearance, tenderness, tolerance, and so on. It doesn't matter whether he has his children two weeks a month or two days. The requirements are the same.

To get an idea of how well you're doing as a single father, answer the questions that follow. Most single fathers at one time or another have to deal with these questions, so if you feel you need help with any of them, you're in good company. And you can get help—just turn to the chapters listed after the questions.

- Do you sometimes wonder whether you want your children at all? (See Chapter 1.)

- Is your separation making you feel angry, miserable, or lonely? (See Chapter 2.)

- Are you afraid your children aren't as close to you as they were before? (See Chapter 3.)

- Do your children complain about their visits to you? (See Chapter 4.)

- Is there still friction and unpleasantness when you deal with your ex-wife? (See Chapter 5.)

- Do your children create problems with your women friends, and vice versa? (See Chapter 6.)

- Have you had problems at your job since your separation? (See Chapter 7.)

- Do you see your children only on weekends? (See Chapter 8.)

- Do you live in a distant city from your children? (See Chapter 9.)

- Do you often find you don't know how to take care of your children's "growing pains"? (See Chapter 10.)

No matter how many problems you may be going through—no matter how discouraged you may sometimes get—there's one thing to remember: where there's pain, there's gain. You can use the pain of separation to help forge a new self-confidence and sense of well-being—to become a more independent person. As single fathers, we may lose court battles, we may lose money, we may lose heart temporarily—but we can also gain *ourselves,* a new person, a new self better than the old self.

There's no way to beat the pain of separation. If anyone offers you a foolproof way out, he's lying. But though you can't beat it, at least you can benefit from it. Since you're going to go through it anyway, you might as well turn it to your advantage.

It's a bit like an operation for a deadly disease: it hurts, but it can save your life. The healing process may be a long one, but it's an absolutely necessary process, and you can't hurry it.

This book doesn't offer any shortcuts. There *are* no shortcuts.

The object of this book is to help you make the most of the healing process, so that your wound heals cleanly and leaves you—and your family—as good as new, or, rather, better than new.

F.F.

ON BEING FATHER

1.

THE GIFT
OF PARENTING

or

How I Became a Single Father

I think I always wanted to be a parent, even back when I was a teenager. It was a need that was always with me. When I was twenty-six, I did become the father of a son, and through the years, parenting has been a tremendous gift to me—a bigger gift than I ever would have thought possible.

Even through the long years of my separation and divorce, being a parent continued to be a gift that sustained me and nourished me—and, I know, set me on the road to being a better person.

Now, whenever I meet men who are going through rotten separations and miserable divorces and don't know what's going to happen to them and their children, I always feel like grabbing them by the shoulders and telling them they must not let go of their children, because being a father may be the best thing that ever happened to them.

I think the parent in me first came out when I was sixteen. That was the year my brother Philip was born. We were a big Italian family living in Brooklyn; there were six children. When Philip was born, my parents were no longer young, and I'm sure they were getting a bit tired of this procession of children. They were only too happy to let some of their responsibility slide onto my shoulders—and I for my part was only too happy to take it. I had discovered in myself an urge to get closer to this small human being who had suddenly entered the family. I don't know where the urge came from; I only know that I found I wanted to be with the baby, to touch him, to smile at him, to comfort him, to be close to him, to take care of him.

Frankly, to love him. For an Italian male in a traditional family in Brooklyn, loving another human being was thought to take just one form: to be a macho stud with women. And while I admit I had plenty of this kind of love in me, I also seemed to have another kind of love in me that wanted to be tender, caring, and nurturing. That's why my little brother Philip was such a great gift to me. He enabled me to express this side of love. Babies are like little gods in Italian families—they're coddled, fussed over, and shamelessly indulged—and so nobody thought it odd or objectionable that I took such an interest in the baby.

If it hadn't been for the baby, one whole side of my nature would have been repressed literally for years to come. I could not have expressed tenderness or caring for any other person without being afraid I'd be laughed at or ridiculed or called a sissy. I couldn't really talk about feelings and emotions with my parents—it just wasn't the way an Italian family operated—and I couldn't talk about them with my girlfriends, either. Or, rather, I was afraid to. Emotions and tenderness were things you simply didn't express. But I *could* express them with a baby.

I became a sort of surrogate parent to Philip. I made a conscious decision that I would always be there for him, always be available to him in a loving way. So, for the next five years, I was probably the person closest to him in the whole world. I became his *amigo*. That's what he called me. When I left for work in the morning, he'd say, "Adiós, amigo." When I got home, he'd say, "Hello, amigo."

Then, when I was twenty-two, I got married. I wanted a family of my own. I wanted children—in fact, I wanted six children, just like my own parents. I loved family. It's a cliché that Italians love their families—and it's true. My family was always very special to me. Even though at times family life was difficult—even though we didn't have a lot of money—even though we fought all the time —we still had each other. The family was a kind of mutual support system. One of the reasons I was attracted to Linda—aside from the fact that she was pretty—was that she also wanted children and that she had all the qualities I'd been taught a wife and mother should have: she was giving, undemanding, altruistic, always there, always helpful.

I wanted to have a family of my own, not to have to "share" my family as I did with Philip. I wanted to be able to do all the things I did for Philip, but to do them with children of my own. I wanted to be able to have all the warm feelings of close, loving relationships around me, to be able to love my children in my own way, to be free to love them without having anyone looking over my shoulder. When my wife became pregnant (we had to wait four years), I was ecstatic. I was very religious at the time, and I prayed for a son (right or wrong, I did want a son). I was also terrified—terrified something would go wrong with the pregnancy. I wanted everything to be perfect. We went to natural childbirth classes and became almost cocky with our new expertise.

Thank goodness, nothing did go wrong, although the doctors shooed me out of the delivery room before the birth occurred. When the nurse finally appeared with a bundle in her arms and said, "Here you are. You're the father of a boy," I was tremendously thankful that everything was okay, that the baby was okay, that Linda was okay. When Linda was wheeled out of the delivery room, she said to me, "Isn't it wonderful? I can't wait to have another one."

I had the perfect family. It was almost a cliché—radiant wife, beautiful son (with his blue eyes and blond hair), beaming grandparents ecstatic with their first grandson, a steady job, a little dream house.

And I was going to be the perfect father—the best father that ever was—better than all the other fathers because I knew all about taking care of a baby and wasn't afraid to be loving and open. I knew how to hold the baby and how to be gentle and delicate with him even though my hands were callused. I knew how to help my wife around the house with the dishes and the cleaning. I wasn't even bothered by changing the dirty diapers, since it gave me a chance to touch the baby.

I was with Christopher every chance I got. Sometimes I even resented Linda because *she* had to have time with the child, too. She nursed the baby, and she preferred to be alone with him during nursing. I was itchy when they were both away from me at such an important time. Still, I was in seventh heaven most of the time, and nothing gave me more pleasure than to lie in bed with Linda while we played with the baby.

Looking back on it now, I realize I was practically a child myself, a child with my real-life doll of a son. I was innocent, inexperienced, and unprepared. I was so full of myself and my pride in my masculine tenderness that I didn't realize how unready I really was to be a father. I had no idea of the responsibility I'd taken on. I didn't know there was more to being a parent than simply loving my son.

I guess I assumed everything would just work out. I'd been taught that everything in life always did work out. Marriage just worked out, sex just worked out—well, parenthood would just work out, too.

My wife, who, like most mothers, was going to carry the major portion of the parenting role, was more concerned than I was, to say the least. She saw that we were both babes in the woods and that we weren't prepared to be parents. She was the one who started to educate herself to be a mother, to study books about breast-feeding, to read Dr. Spock. At the time, I didn't like to read at all, much less to read books by supposed experts on bringing up children. I figured that simple common sense would see me through my child-rearing responsibilities.

I never saw the worries that afflicted her, the responsibilities that weighed on her when she thought of the task we'd undertaken. What did I do? I role-played. We both role-played, really, but Linda had some idea of what we were doing, while my role was limited mainly to lending all-purpose moral support. I became the Daddy/Provider and the Disciplinarian, just as all fathers were "supposed" to do. Linda was the Patient Mother. I gloried in my role, just as I gloried in my son.

It all fell apart when Christopher was six and Linda finally decided she had to get away to be alone and think about things. She needed "space"—she knew she'd gotten boxed into the roles we'd been playing, and she wanted to rescue herself before her own identity got swamped entirely. That was the beginning of our separation, and we never got back together. The marriage had been pretty rocky for quite a while, and now, in retrospect, I can see that it was hardly surprising that it came to an end.

I was still wearing my Ideal Father robes, and when my wife moved, I resolved that the household would go on just as before. I'd be *both* parents to my son—mother and father together. I knew (or thought I knew) I could do it. I knew how to cook, clean, and do the housework—in fact, I was almost better at it than Linda. The day she left, I calmly told Chris he could go play with his friends and that the Sunday meal—the traditional Italian afternoon macaroni—would be ready as usual at three o'clock.

I accepted the separation calmly, like the strong man I supposedly was. I wasn't going to panic. I wasn't going to let it affect me. Everything was going to go on just as it always had. We'd simply ignore our feelings and go on with our lives.

This lasted four days, and then I fell apart. I hit bottom. I was a wreck and I couldn't conceal the fact any longer. I finally had to begin to face myself, and I realized how bottled up I was and how trapped in traditional clichés I was.

And it was then that being a parent gave me its second great gift. The first had come in letting me express love openly to another human being. Now my status as a parent suddenly and overwhelmingly made me realize the extent and weight of my responsibilities. It began to show me how unprepared I was to really bring up a child. I'd been just coasting along in my rosy cliché role, not realizing how little true contact I was having with my son or my wife.

To put it bluntly, being a parent showed me my failings. Or rather, being a *single* parent showed me. I never would have learned this lesson if my wife and I had stayed together and gone on as we were. It was only in becoming a single parent that I saw how much I had to learn and was kicked into trying to improve myself. It was painful. And frightening. But I can see that it was absolutely necessary. I don't like to think what would have happened to Christopher—or to me—if something hadn't jolted me out of my rut. I hadn't realized that I was dug into a hole. I was even less trained for separation than I had been for marriage. Fortunately, I went into therapy for a while, and so did Christopher—and that helped a lot.

When I started to pick up the pieces, I saw that I just couldn't go on being the kind of stereotype I'd slipped into in my marriage. The separation forced me really to look at myself, to examine myself and admit that I was less than a whole person.

It was then that I began the long, slow process of trying to make a whole person of myself—that is, to simply try to be myself. That's what single parenthood really did for me: it made me a person. It really was a gift, though a painful gift.

For ten months Christopher was with me alone and I was a full-time parent. It was a baptism by fire. I was plunged into it with no real preparation. There was no respite. I was responsible for him just about all the time. There was no time to rest. There was nobody to help, nobody I could turn to and say, "I'm tired. You take over. You take him for a while." There was no way to go off by myself when I felt impatient or when I was depressed. I could hardly even deal with my *own* feelings—and here I was having to be available constantly to a demanding six-year-old with feelings of his own.

I could see I really had to work on myself. There was so much I knew I'd have to change in myself, so much I'd have to learn: how to be patient, how to control my anger and not vent it on my son, how to continue to function when I felt utterly powerless, how to keep my insecurities from affecting my son.

I was determined not to lose my son as I'd lost my wife. I knew I couldn't give him up or live without him—ever. He was too important a part of my life. (And I, for better or worse, was too important a part of his.) I knew I couldn't live without having him around. Without tucking him in every night as I had since he was a baby. Without telling him his bedside story (not a story in a book, but a made-up story). Without rubbing his back to get rid of his knots. All those things that I depended on so utterly. But in order to maintain a life with my son, it was obvious I'd have to become a more competent parent—a more *real* parent—than I had been.

I had to start on a conscious campaign to correct myself. I was grateful to find out I *could* correct myself, that it was possible to change. I suddenly knew how Linda must have felt six years ago when she came home from the hospital with the new baby and saw how unprepared she was to be a mother. She knew she had to start learning. Now I saw I had to start learning how to be a father. I had to do all the things I'd scorned six years ago, all the things I'd felt were "below" me: read up on child care—talk to other parents —learn about how to raise a child.

And I did make progress, slow but sure. Most of the people I talked with were women. But then by chance I was introduced to a single fathers' group. A social worker at my job told me about it. It was a revelation. I discovered other men who were really interested in being fathers, who liked being tender, loving, and caring. (Men I didn't have to be embarrassed with. That was important.) But the most important thing was to see that these other men were able to be absolutely successsful single fathers. With them as examples, I began to be a more competent full-time parent.

When those ten months were over, Linda and I worked out a separation arrangement in which we each had Chris for alternate two-week periods. And that has continued to the present time. The process of trying to improve myself has continued, too, and I suspect will never stop, since I never manage to be the ideal father I have in my mind's eye.

The gift of parenting has continued to manifest itself in other ways.

It has brought back to me my own childhood, or, rather, brought back all those things in myself that had gotten buried under the weight of my role-playing. By watching my son, by playing with him, by just having him around, those buried things began to resurface—taking pleasure in simple things; being open and honest; doing things on the spur of the moment; taking chances; not worrying about being vulnerable. It's as though I'd had restored to me a whole part of myself that I'd lost. The worst thing is that I hadn't even realized I'd lost it. But now I had it back, and it was a tremendous gift.

Then there was the even more valuable gift of having an absolutely unique one-on-one relationship with another person. And I
mean absolutely unique. Nobody can be what I am to my son;
nobody can be what he is to me. Being a parent—a *single* parent—
has given me the opportunity for this closeness with my son. If I
were still married, I'd have a different kind of closeness with him.
It would be a closeness in which his mother shared, and while I'm
certainly not knocking it, it wouldn't be the same. It gives us a kind
of sharing in which we get sustenance and support from each
other. And the benefits flow equally both ways. That's what I mean
when I say it's a one-on-one relationship. My son gives me as much
as I give him. We give each other different things, of course, but we
each get equal amounts of support from the relationship.

Chris tells me things he wouldn't tell another human being.
When he was in therapy for a while five years ago, I'd say to him,
"Tell your therapist what's bothering you—that's what he's there
for." And Chris would say to me, "Daddy, it's too personal. I'd
rather talk to you about it." And he has continued to talk to me
about the things that are close to him—his problems, his doubts,
his pleasures, and just the ordinary things that are on his mind.
When he goes away to camp, his letters to me continue the closeness. Perhaps in one letter he'll ask for advice (for instance, some
boys in his cabin are assholes and are annoying and hurting him).
I'll write back and maybe suggest a course of action he could try
(like taking one of them aside and telling him honestly how he has
been hurting Chris). Chris will write to me and be blunt about how
things turned out (my advice was a flop and Chris had to deal with
the problem another way). It provides a mutual give-and-take that
neither of us could duplicate in exactly the same way with any
other person.

Then there are the smaller, unspoken kinds of communication
that connect him to me—the watch he forgets on his bureau and
that goes bleep-bleep every hour and reminds me of him; the
socks he always leaves on the floor and that I always yell about; the
wet towel he left in the bedroom the first time he went off to camp
and that I didn't touch for two months, so it would be a reminder
of him. All these things are gifts of being a parent that I cherish.

I always think I was lucky as a single father: I never had to ask myself, at the time of my separation, if I really wanted to keep my son. I *knew* I wanted to keep him. There was no question—no question at all. I wasn't like some fathers who really do have to consider the question. I've met some men who did elect to stop seeing their children altogether. I can't empathize in any way with their decision, but I have to give them credit for having truly thought the thing through and made the decision that was right for *them*.

But I'll still come down on the side of parenthood every time. Living with a child is, literally, an incomparable experience. It's a gift that has made my life what it is today.

I couldn't live without it.

2.

AFTER SEPARATION, BEFORE DIVORCE

*Getting Through the Hard Parts
of the Separation Period
Without Wrecking
Your Future or Your Family*

To start with, we'll make a few assumptions:

You've moved out.

You've found a new place to live.

You consider your marriage definitely finished.

You and your wife have agreed to get a divorce.

You love your children deeply and want to stay close to them.

At this point in your life, your main concern is: what do you do to make the best of your single-again existence? In particular, how do you maintain your close relationship with your children in the face of your separation? How do you remain the father to your children that you've always been?

That's what this book is about.

This is not a book about how to survive the traumas of divorce, or how to get custody of your children, or how to start meeting women again. It's about how to continue being a father to your children after you've separated from your wife, in spite of all the changes you're going through. It's an offering of options to promote hope and self-actualization as a nurturing male parent.

This book concentrates on this one topic: you and your children. You won't find much here about the legal side of separation and divorce, or the money angle. And as for the emotional side, we'll go into the tangled web of your id only insofar as it affects your relationship with your family.

Okay. Having gotten that out of the way. . . .

GETTING OFF ON THE RIGHT FOOT:
THINGS TO DO *NOW*
IF YOU HAVEN'T ALREADY DONE THEM

There's usually a relatively long separation period between the time you actually leave your wife (or she leaves you) and the time the divorce decree comes through. In my own case, it was almost four years: Linda moved out in 1979 and we were legally divorced in 1982. Most of the other divorced men I've met through the years have had separation periods in the eighteen-month range, although they've varied from six months to six years.

It's an extremely important period. It lays the foundation for your whole future. If you don't get off on the right foot now, you may run into a lot of trouble later. The problem is that the separation period is usually so chaotic, disorganized, and traumatic that it's hard to think straight, much less to make sane and rational decisions about the future.

But there are a few things you should attend to as early as possible in the separation. If you've already been separated six months and you haven't attended to them—or even if you're already divorced—you should try to remedy the matter as soon as you can. Better late than never.

See your children regularly. If, during the roller-coaster ride of separation, you've let yourself get out of touch with your children, don't wait—get back in touch. The separation period sets the tone for the divorce, and if you stay out of touch, it'll be all the harder in court to make an effective case for yourself. It's hard to ask for shared custody, for instance, if all through the separation period you've hardly seen your children at all.

The best way to prevent this problem is not to let it get started in the first place. If you establish a visiting routine with your children from the moment of separation, then it will be ingrained by the time of the divorce, and your ex-wife will have a hard time pulling any shenanigans with you about custody. Most separated men *do* want to see their children, but they're prevented from doing so by two headaches:

1. They're so glad to be away from their wives that they can't stand the idea of going back there, even to see the children.

2. They feel guilty about having moved out—they feel it somehow puts them in the wrong—and so they let their wives intimidate them into staying away from the children.

If you find yourself having either of these two reactions, *squash them*. They lead to nothing but trouble.

In the first place, your children *need* to see you. A father's nurturing is vitally important to kids. Even if your wife is, pardon me, a bitch on wheels, don't let dislike of her keep you from your children. You may feel depressed about the idea of going back to the house, but think how depressed your kids will be without you. Kids need routine and continuity. You've upset the routine of their lives by moving out. The least you can do is visit them regularly, like clockwork, so that they have something to depend on. They need to know that you haven't abandoned them. Even if you and your wife have agreed that she'll have the children for the first month of the separation and you'll have them for the second, visit them on weekends during that first month. Keep your hand in.

In the second place, the fact that you were the one who moved out doesn't make you the "guilty" party. It takes two to tango. Both spouses are responsible for the separation (well, usually, anyway). You're still the children's father, and you have as much right to them as your wife does. You shouldn't lay a guilt trip on yourself or let your wife lay one on you. You have every right to visit the children as often as you like. Also, the house is still *your* house. There's no reason you shouldn't go back to live in it occasionally. Let your wife go visit her mother for a couple of weeks, and *you* stay with the children. (Don't worry that you won't be able to cope; you'd manage to cope if you were still married and your wife, say, went into the hospital for two weeks; so you can cope now.)

Show your children where you live. Kids don't have abstract imaginations. They operate in the here and now; they only understand specifics. When you move out, it'll seem to them as if you've more or less evaporated. The younger the children are, the less they'll understand where you've gone. They'll also be beset by all sorts of fears for your safety—they'll worry that you don't have a place to sleep at night, that you don't have anything to eat, that there's no one to do your laundry, that you're going to die. You owe it to them to relieve their minds about all this. Show them where you live; take them there for a visit as soon as possible after your separation from your wife. This will help them "pin you down" in their minds; it will give them something concrete to hold on to.

ADDED BENEFIT: they'll be more likely to phone you frequently at your new home if they have a mental picture of the place they're reaching.

Show them that you have a bed to sleep on and a refrigerator with plenty of food to eat. If you've just moved into the apartment and there is no bed (yet) and the refrigerator isn't full of food, then get the children involved in the planning of the apartment.

"The bed is being delivered on Friday. Where do you think I should put it—along this wall, or under the window?"

"The refrigerator is still empty. Let's go on a shopping trip to the supermarket this afternoon, and you can help me load up on provisions."

"There's a phone in the living room. Do you think I should get another one for the bedroom so I can talk to you at home while I'm lying in bed?"

The children should get the idea that they'll be visiting you in the new place regularly. It will be part of *their* lives as well as of yours. Be as specific about this as you can. "I'll pick you up every Friday afternoon after school and we'll spend the weekend here until Sunday night." Even if you and your wife haven't yet agreed on a schedule for sharing the children, at least let them know they'll be visiting you again soon. "I'll call you on Tuesday—five days from now—and we'll plan your next visit."

A few other things to do to get them involved in your new place:

Assign them a personal "territory," a place in the apartment of their own—a room if possible, or a closet, or even just a drawer in a bureau. "This is *your* drawer. It's just for you—not for anybody else. You can put whatever you want in it, and it'll stay just the way you left it until the next time you're here."

Have something of theirs in the apartment. "I like that picture you drew of the castle. Let's put it up on the bedroom wall."

Bring a few items or pieces of furniture from your house to the new place—a sofa, an armchair, a dining table, a couple of pictures. They'll help take the edge of strangeness off your abode; the children will find it more comforting and familiar, less strange and threatening. "How do you like the old table? It fits just right here, doesn't it?"

Cool it with your wife. You probably won't want to see much of her now that you've moved out. Even if you long for her occasionally, you probably realize the impracticality and pain of seeing her. That's all to the good—it'll help put a damper on all the frictions and disagreements that led to the breakup in the first place. You may also be angry at her, frustrated, vengeful, or violent. These feelings must be discharged—but privately. Don't act on them with your wife. (Sometimes it'll seem as if this requires a superhuman effort, but the passage of time will make it easier.)

Treat the separation period as a cooling-off time. The safest procedure is to see as little of your wife as possible. Later, you can start to think about fashioning some sort of practical working relationship with her. Right now the principal consideration is simply to avoid friction, in particular to avoid any actions that might end up doing irreparable damage to you.

Translated into practical terms, this means:

Don't go whole hog on lawyers. You'll need a lawyer, yes, but keep it as simple and straightforward as possible. If you have fantasies of raking your wife over the coals in the courtroom, wait a month before hiring a lawyer to carry them out. Ten to one, you're getting in over your head—and you'll only end up with a huge pile of legal fees, a lot of headaches, and very little real satisfaction.

Communicate with your wife by mail. If the two of you are on bad terms, this may be easier than meeting in person.

Don't make threats. "I'll kidnap the children if you try to keep them from me." "I'll kill that no-good boyfriend of yours." "My lawyers will make such a hash of you that you won't know what hit you." You may feel like saying these things, but don't. They have a habit of boomeranging. They give your wife ammunition to use against you. For instance, if she can legitimately claim in court that you threatened her, then you'll suddenly find you have a lot of explaining to do as to your qualifications as a responsible parent.

Get help. If you're really hurting, get counseling. Believe me, it'll save you a lot of heartache in the long run. Any kind of counseling is better than none—a single fathers' group; a therapist; a social worker; a minister or priest. It's not so much whom you see or what they say—it's just that you have some impartial human contact that takes you out of yourself and gives you a means of sounding off. Counseling is the best possible means of releasing your feelings and still keeping a liking for yourself, while you get back into shape to act rationally again.

Contact the children's school. Get in touch with the school and tell them that you and your wife are now living apart. Give the school authorities your new address and phone number. Ask that they list your name as well as your wife's on all school record forms, and request that they mail you copies of school reports and your children's report cards.

Most schools will do this as a matter of course. A few haven't yet gotten used to the idea that people *do* get divorced and will ask you all sorts of questions about where the child's "real" home is. Say that the children have two homes . . . and keep saying it until it sinks in.

Exchange all phone numbers. Everybody in the family should have everyone else's phone numbers. Especially both your wife *and* your children should know your numbers (both your work number and the number of your new abode). If the children are young—too young to remember telephone numbers—give them little address books of their own. You want to be sure that they have the means and the ability to call you at any time if they need you. If you fear that they may be afraid to call you while they're with their mother, teach them how to use pay phones, and tell them that in an emergency they can always ask their teacher or principal at school to call you for them.

Try to get company benefits. Your place of work may have special benefits that you, as a separated or divorced man, can qualify for. Since every little bit of assistance helps during this period, it pays to poke around.

Hardship pay. Separation—and the subsequent extra expenses that inevitably come along on its coattails—may fall under the category of "hardship," thus entitling you to some assistance with your paycheck.

Counseling or therapy. If you need help on the mental front, your company package of medical benefits will often include some provision for psychiatric counseling or other care.

Child care. Few companies actually have child-care facilities on the premises, but some (more and more every year) include some sort of child-care benefits in their pay package, for the use of divorced employees of either sex.

Scheduling. If you usually work the night shift and it's driving you crazy now that you're separated and alone, then you can often arrange some sort of switch to a more convenient arrangement.

Get support. For most men, the worst part of separation is the fact that they feel so depressed so often. Even if you're happy to be out of a disastrous marriage, you can't help feeling awful that it's over.

Being alone so much now, you're a perfect prey to depression, guilt, and despondency.

What you need is moral support from other people. There's nothing like a big circle of friends and acquaintances to lift you out of the doldrums—to listen to your tale of woe, to provide shoulders for you to cry on, to offer sympathy.

Don't be reluctant to ask for support. The old macho image of the strong silent man suffering in silence should be thrown to the dogs. If you try to live up to this old standard, you'll be strong and silent and *miserable*. In my view, it's a lot better to admit frankly that you're in pain and ask for help. You'll then get a good dose of bucking up, which will make you feel a million times better.

Don't go just anywhere for support and emotional stroking. You want to be sure you'll meet a receptive ear, not a cold shoulder.

WHERE TO LOOK FOR SUPPORT

Single-parent groups. These are excellent, because you know they'll be sympathetic to you. You may not get along with everybody in the group, but there will be enough kindred spirits to make it worth your while. You'll also see that you're not alone in your misery—there's always someone else who's even more miserable than you are.

People at work. Often this is a fertile field. You'll have to pick with care, but a good friend at work, male or female, is worth his or her weight in gold. Those eight hours from nine to five can seem like an eternity when you're depressed, and a friend at arm's reach can help you get through those long daily stints.

Friends. Again, you have to be selective. Now that you're separated, you'll find that some old friends draw away from you; they feel they have to choose between you and your wife—and they choose her. Lean on the friends who stick with *you.*

Clubs. Join a club that interests you. The members may not give you actual emotional support (at first), but at least they'll involve you in an activity that you like, and that will help take your mind off your troubles.

Women. Now that you're separated, you're on the free market again, so to speak, and you'll probably avail yourself of the opportunity to meet a lot of women. You'll inevitably find some who are the mothering type. They'll provide a willing ear for you to talk to —at least for a while, unless you abuse the privilege and really talk their ears off.

Divorced men. Some of them will be willing to listen to you, having been through the trauma of divorce themselves. Others will try to stay as far away from the subject as possible.

WHERE NOT TO LOOK FOR SUPPORT

Relatives. Most relatives do more harm than good. No matter how much so-called sympathy they may give you, under the surface there always seems to be an annoying undercurrent of pity, resentment, or scorn. "I told you your marriage would never last." "You poor man, I feel so sorry for you." "You've made a real mess of your life, haven't you." "You've disgraced the family." "Tell me, was Ida involved with another man?" "Who, *you two?* But *why?*"

Male friends. Most married and single friends will tend to feel awkward around you. They want you to be your same old self. They'll be embarrassed by your current state and they won't want to talk about it.

Your children. A definite no-no. Your children are the last people you should go to for sympathy. The less they see of your misery and confusion, the better. They need understanding themselves— and they may need it more than you do. They are not equipped to *give* it. To say things like, "Daddy's so sad this morning, don't bother me," or "I'm so glad I've still got *you,*" or "Now that Mommy's gone, you'll have to be real nice to Daddy," is unfair to the children. It's putting a burden on them that they can't shoulder. (You'll slip occasionally, but that's no reason not to try your damnedest to avoid the pitfall.)

Dealing with Your Emotions

Women don't have a corner on the emotion market when it comes to separation and divorce. Men, and especially fathers, get the same one-way ticket to trauma time as women do. The image of the divorced man as a liberated playboy shaking off his marriage like an old shirt is a myth. (If only it were as easy and as painless as that!)

It's a rare man who doesn't feel one (or usually more) of the following emotions during his separation:

guilt
loneliness
anger
depression
sense of failure
abandonment

Nobody wants to feel these emotions, but they have a way of creeping up and snaring us before we know what's happening to us.

Why try to keep them under control at all? Why not just give in to them and have all that nice gratifying anger and self-pity? Why not let go completely? Why not give a free rein to your anger and have the pleasure of lashing out at everybody? Why not let the tears of self-pity drip and get lots of sympathy from others? Because . . . there's a certain delicate line between accepting emotions and giving in to them. Give in to them and you may sink deeper and deeper into mental instability. Accept them and you can discharge them properly and learn more about yourself in the process.

Then there's the most practical consideration: letting your emotions get out of control can screw up your whole future with your children. Too much guilt, loneliness, anger, depression, or sense of failure or abandonment will end up scarring either you or them. Too much anger can lead to violence—violence that sooner or later gets out of bounds and begins to be aimed at those who really have no part in it, that is, your children. Too much guilt may ruin you for any future healthy relationships with women. And too much loneliness or depression can lead you to ignore your children or lose your job. For the sake of your children as well as for yourself, you should try to avoid acting on your harmful feelings.

As men, many of us were never taught how to deal with emotional feelings. We were encouraged to be strong, to compete, to "succeed"—which usually meant we had to strive to keep a pretty rigid control over ourselves. This control often breaks down under the stresses of separation and divorce, and we may be as helpless as babies in trying to deal with it. Either we grow up and learn to deal with the problems, or we let a big part of ourselves get flushed down the drain.

Guilt. Guilt is inevitable. Everybody feels it, so don't worry that you're the only one. Guilt about hurting or abandoning your wife probably won't bother you as much as guilt about hurting and abandoning your children. The children are innocent parties in your breakup, and they're being hurt gratuitously, whereas your wife contributed materially to the separation, and therefore you may not feel quite so sorry for her. But the children . . . you'll wonder whether you were right to break up. Will it hurt the children? Will you see enough of them? Will you neglect them? Are they blaming you?

OPTIONS: Time is the best antidote for guilt; it will fade eventually in the normal course of events. Meanwhile, while you're waiting for it to do so, the next best thing is a good healthy dose of realism. Specifically, be realistic about your needs versus the children's needs. It's a case of "What do I owe myself?" versus "What do I owe them?" Sure, the children are miserable after you move out, but so are you. And you and they might be even more miserable if you'd stuck it out with your wife. They may be hurt now that you're separated, but you might have gone insane if you'd stayed married. Accept that it's over and done with. You decided to break with your wife . . . it was the best thing to do . . . the chips have to fall where they may . . . the children will have to make the best of it.

For children, the tensions before the separation are usually worse than the split-up itself. Staying together "for the kids' sake" often does more harm than good.

Depression. Depression is lethargy, disorientation, confusion, hopelessness, lack of interest in anything, boredom on the job, not being able to get out of bed in the morning. It comes and goes. It's the dark side of the diabolical manic-depressive duo: wild exhilaration one day, utter gloom the next. It's caused by the fact that you're in the midst of a change that's too big to absorb all at once. You've got emotional changes, physical changes (a new home), and often financial changes happening all at once. It's enough to get anybody down. Your overworked mental system simply opts out of the problem and leaves you in an emotional no-man's-land. You've left the past, but you haven't arrived yet in the future.

OPTIONS: The best antidote is plain old activity, especially physical activity. Your brain doesn't have time to dwell completely on your misery if you're in the middle of a game of handball or swinging a bat or sanding the floor or dashing around the kitchen as you fix a meal for six people. Once you're depressed, it's hard to drag yourself up for an activity, so the smartest thing is to schedule activities ahead of time, so that you're absolutely obligated to do them.

Loneliness. You feel miserably alone . . . nobody notices you . . . the phone never rings . . . you've got a whole evening to face with nothing to do (and it's only six o'clock) . . . the children are gone until next week . . . there's nothing to do but stare at blank walls . . . you see couples together on the street and feel like you're going to cry. Loneliness isn't as dangerous as some other emotions, especially anger and depression, but it sure as hell makes life unpleasant. I think it's the toughest emotion of all to face. So many of us have never lived alone at all—we've gone right from our parents' house into marriage—that we have no experience to help us cope with it.

OPTIONS: Lean on your friends. Don't sit home alone. Do something with people. If you don't have any friends, or your friends are busy, then go to a movie. Don't romanticize the memory of your marriage; it wasn't a nonstop smorgasbord of jolly companionship; there were plenty of times when you were lonely even during your marriage (admit it!). Sex can also be an antidote to loneliness, but it's a two-edged sword. Good sex can banish all traces of loneliness, but a sour one-night stand can leave you feeling more lonely than before. Another hint: don't live in a dump. A dreary home only adds to your misery. If you have to be home alone, at least let that home be cheery; beg your mother or a friend to decorate it a bit if you don't know how yourself.

Anger. Anger is dangerous because, unlike other emotions, it can hurt others as well as yourself. It's also practically unavoidable because it tends to be a sort of all-purpose response to all the other emotions. Sometimes you're angry at your wife: she seems like a betrayer, a money-grubber, or a conniver. Sometimes you're angry simply at things in general: you made an investment in the American Dream—a wife, a car, children—and the dream betrayed you. Wherever the anger comes from, acting on it is dangerous because it can hurt your children as well as yourself. You may be angry at your wife or at things in general, but you may end up screaming and shouting at the children because they're the only people around. There's some excuse for letting yourself be hurt by emotion, but there's no excuse at all for hurting others.

OPTIONS: Of all emotion, anger seems to be the most difficult to deal with. You can make all sorts of resolutions—"I'm going to keep my temper, I'm not going to let myself get mad all the time, I'm not going to yell at people"—but these feelings have to get out somehow; it's the only healthy thing. How? The classic (almost corny) male way is to go out and punch a wall. As a policeman, though, I've found that punching hard objects is not the answer. Frankly, I prefer a more difficult outlet: crying. Then there's kicking, screaming, and the like, but if you're that bad off, I'd suggest treating yourself to counseling. As soon as your anger starts getting out of hand, get professional help. You can't afford to trifle with this. You've got to get some sort of treatment for your anger if it leads to violence. If you find yourself uncontrollably yelling at your children, that's indication enough that you need help. If you don't know where to go for therapy, ask somebody (a minister, a priest, a social worker, a librarian, a school guidance counselor, a friend, Ann Landers) to direct you. If you're ashamed or embarrassed to ask, grit your teeth and *ask anyway*. It takes guts, but it's worth it.

Sense of abandonment. Even if you were the one who physically walked out of the house, you may feel that your family abandoned *you*. You feel discarded, useless, left behind, out in the cold . . . while your wife and the children forge ahead as a unit. There's no one to care for you, cook for you, cater to you, soothe you, and (let's admit it) mother you. This is a bad blow to your sense of self-worth. It leads to those questions that you may never have understood before but now understand all too well: "What am I doing here?" "Why am I alive?" "What's the point of it all?"

OPTIONS: The best thing you can do is see your children regularly. This will prove that you still have a family and haven't been entirely left behind. Over the longer term, you can work at being more self-sufficient so that you don't automatically go to pieces when the family isn't circulating around you like electrons around an atom.

Danger Symptoms

The trouble with emotions is that they can get out of hand without you realizing it. It's hard to keep a clear perspective about yourself, especially during a turbulent time like your separation. (It's always easier to have a clear perspective about other people than about yourself!) So if you begin to go overboard with harmful emotions, you won't always realize it. It feels so good to indulge your emotions—like scratching a particularly annoying itch. Even supposedly unpleasant emotions like depression and loneliness can give a sort of perverse satisfaction since they make it possible to wallow in self-pity and self-justification. Most of the time, men who are in this position don't realize how badly out of kilter their psyches are. They need guideposts to tell them where they stand.

Here is a list of danger symptoms. If you recognize any of them in yourself, be warned: it's time to get help.

thoughts of suicide

thoughts of murder

violent fantasies ("I'll slap some sense into her")

thinking about how to get revenge

accident proneness

deep depression that lasts for more than a few days

illness or physical symptoms that seem to have no obvious cause

obsessive dependence on lawyers ("Don't talk to me! See my lawyer!")

Establish priorities. Hoard what little energy you have. If one week your job has to be the number-one priority, then don't bother about making the bed or doing the laundry or talking to the lawyers or cooking a big dinner with the kids. If another time—on a weekend, for instance—the kids are the number-one priority, then put your job out of your mind and forget about doing the shopping and don't tell your wife you'll meet her to discuss the divorce.

And keep some time for yourself. Don't say, "But I have no time. The kids need me . . . my job needs me . . . the lawyers need me . . ." *You* need you. You should have first call on your own time. Don't keep running all the time. If you don't already have an hour or two a day to call your own, then get ruthless and make time. Take the phone off the hook; put your feet up.

Through even the worst periods, don't worry too much about the children. Don't neglect them; but on the other hand, don't flagellate yourself about their condition. They're more resilient than you are. You may be flailing yourself with worry about how they're going to survive the divorce and how your actions have affected them. Don't. If you worry too much, the kids will sense your worry, and this will only make them worse off. (What they want most is a father who is not at his wit's end with misery.) If you paint the situation bleakly, they'll perceive it bleakly. But if you manage not to be too tense, uptight, and fraught, they'll relax and feel a whole lot better about the situation.

How to Keep Heavy Emotions from Disrupting Your Life

I'd be the last person to say there are any easy ways to get through spells of emotional heavy weather. I speak from experience. I was an emotional mess during the several months that followed my separation. I cried myself to sleep many a night. I had strange nightmares. I couldn't concentrate on my job. I'd break out in a cold sweat at the most inopportune moments.

There didn't seem to be anyone I could really talk to about this. I made a couple of attempts to talk seriously with some of my male friends, but most of them seemed more interested in playing handball or having a drink than in listening to my emotional tale of woe. I also approached some of my women friends, but the ones who were willing to listen seemed more interested in mothering me than in giving me any positive feedback.

I finally ended up (through a long series of coincidences) in the office of my former college psychology teacher. I hadn't seen him in a year or two, but he'd been a good friend to me in college, and he seemed the one person I could rely on to give me good objective advice.

He calmed me down and gave me a talking-to that helped put me back on an even keel. He didn't have any miracle cures or magic wands that would wave away the problems and pain. In fact, he warned me that in the long run, it would probably do more harm than good to try any tricky evasive maneuvers to escape my troubles. His main point was that though you can never escape the emotions themselves, at least you can prevent yourself from being incapacitated by them—and making a mess of your life in the process.

He gave me four pieces of advice for getting through the mine field of the separation period without going down with the ship. To this day, they're still the best advice I've ever heard on the subject. Here they are;

Don't Make Big Decisions When You're in an Emotional Mess

In the early days of separation—and even for months afterward —it's natural to be on an emotional roller coaster, down in the depths one day, up on the heights the next, bouncing back and forth between anger and depression, rage and despair, elation and guilt.

This is natural—and painful.

When you're on the roller coaster, the up cycle with its euphoria and exhilaration can be just as dangerous as the down cycle with its gloom and depression. Both cycles cloud your judgment. Even if you think you're clearheaded and rational, chances are that you're not.

It's dangerous to make important decisions when you're in one of these states. If you do make decisions, you often make the wrong ones—and regret them later on. If it's at all possible, postpone decisions until you're sailing in calmer waters—particularly important decisions like whether to do any of these:

> fight your wife for custody of the children
> move
> hire lawyers and go to court
> quit your job or ask for a raise
> remarry

You may say, "Sure, it sounds sensible to keep a low profile when you're in an emotional stew, but how do you actually know when you're in such a state?" Often you don't know. It's not always easy to recognize that you're under emotional stress. You may think you're okay when actually you're almost off the wall. Of course, if you're depressed all the time, or angry all the time, there's not much doubt that you're off balance emotionally. But it's not always so clear-cut. A couple of indicator questions may be helpful here.

> Have you been having bad dreams?
> Have you been crying a lot?
> Do you have an "empty" feeling? Do you "feel nothing"?
> Do you have a hard time forcing yourself to get up
>   in the morning?
> Are you having a hard time concentrating on your job?
> Do you brood about your wife all the time?
> Do you talk about your wife and your
>   separation whenever you're with people?

A yes answer to any of these questions indicates that your emotions are not exactly placid. (In other words, you're in the same boat as most other recently separated fathers.) And if two or more of them are yeses, you can be pretty sure you're off balance emotionally.

You may be in a state of emotional overload, which is almost like a mini–nervous breakdown. If it goes on too long, it becomes a genuine nervous breakdown. Like an overloaded electric circuit, you've simply blown a fuse and ceased to function for a while. The best thing you can do is simply recognize that you are emotionally overloaded. Tell yourself, "This is a state of too much emotion. That's all. I'm not going crazy. I'm not losing my mind. I'm not developing a complex. This is temporary." And don't be surprised at your lack of energy, ambition, and drive. You're using so much psychic energy in being miserable and worried that you have very little left for getting through normal daily activities.

Emotional overload is the enemy of responsibility. It's hard to take any kind of responsibility—that is, to make any important decisions—when you're short-circuiting from too many emotions of various kinds. It follows that you should try to avoid as much responsibility as possible during this period. This may sound cowardly, gutless, and unmanly, but it's better than the alternative of accepting too much responsibility and then botching it.

BASIC RULE: If you can possibly let it slide, do so.

This is a total reversal of the proverb, Do it now. When you're emotionally overloaded, you should *not* do it now. On the contrary, put it off. There will be plenty of time later to tighten the reins and get your act back together. For now, simple survival is all you're aiming for.

This state *will* pass. Like a storm, it just has to be ridden out. Meanwhile, don't try to force big changes in your life or make important decisions. Wait for the calm after the storm. If circumstances force you to make crucial decisions at this time, move carefully. At least try not to make the decisions until you've talked it over with a friend or, better, a professional such as a psychologist or a counselor—someone you can trust to keep his head on his shoulders and tell you frankly whether you're making a good choice.

Try to Figure Out What You Really Want

This is important for "keeping your head together." In the early days of separation, you may be pretty confused about exactly what you're trying to accomplish or where you're trying to get to. You'll often find yourself in the odd position of simultaneously holding two opposite opinions. For instance:

You miss your wife . . . but you don't ever want to see her again.

You don't want to pay child support . . . but you do want to provide for your kids.

You miss your kids . . . but you can't stand the trouble and pain of going home to visit them.

This is normal. Irrational, yes. But normal. It happens because you're trying to go in two directions at once. You've got one foot still in marriage, the other in single fatherhood—and they're playing tug-of-war with you.

The sooner you start to sort out this confusion, the better. It's not something you can resolve in a day (or even in a week or a month, necessarily), but it's important to start.

As an example, let's assume you've said to yourself, "I miss my wife . . . but I don't ever want to see her again." (This is an awfully common reaction among newly separated men, by the way. I said it; most of my separated friends said it; I suspect separated fathers will go on saying it forever.) Of course, the statement is a complete contradiction: you can't logically want and not want your wife simultaneously.

Instead of muddling along in the shadow of this contradiction, it pays to try to get to the root of it and straighten it out in your head. Once you start thinking over this particular problem, you can come to one of two conclusions: (1) You really do miss your wife, and you do want to see her again; or (2) you really don't want to see her anymore—you may miss having a wife, but you don't really miss this particular woman. Whatever you decide, you'll be less confused and less frustrated. You'll have a good basis for taking further action—either in trying to get together again with your wife or in deciding to make the split final by going ahead with the divorce.

Once you've made up your mind as to what you really want, the only problem you've got to worry about is backsliding. The old confusions can creep up on you when you're not looking. Be on guard. Whenever you find yourself slipping into a depression, you'll know what to say to pull yourself out of it: "I've already been over this. I know what I want and why I want it. I don't have to flounder through the whole problem again."

The trick is to know what your priorities are and stick to them. If you've figured out what you really want, then you won't get depressed over what you *think* you want. It saves a lot of wear and tear on the nerves.

Don't Do What Feels Good, Do What Is Good

It's the easiest thing in the world to run wild after you've gotten separated. Suddenly your wife is gone—your marriage is gone—all your constraints are gone. There's nothing to restrain you. You're on a field day. Sexual sprees are one common result—new women every week, dates every night, casual pickups whenever the urge hits you. Or the emotional spree can take other forms—orgies of overeating, pigging out on brownies, pizza, or junk food; compulsive movie-going; even negative forms of self-indulgence like arguing day-in day-out with your wife.

These things may feel good (temporarily), but they're not good for you. It's the kid-in-the-candy-store syndrome. The candy tastes awfully good, but it leaves you with a bellyache.

Any kind of sensual or emotional overindulgence eventually turns into false pleasure—it leaves you feeling worse than you did before. It doesn't solve anything. It only postpones the day of reckoning. It's a way of pushing problems out of sight so they won't have to be faced.

It's not exactly easy to get up and leave the candy store just when you're about to reach for a gallon of ice cream, but it pays to try.

PRACTICAL EXERCISE: Make a list of the ten things that give you the most pleasure in life. They can be anything—companionship, conversation, sex, bowling, hanging out at the local bar. As best you can, rank them in the order of their importance to you, from one to ten. Be as truthful as possible. You're trying to decide what really does give you pleasure, not what just seems to give you pleasure. Once you've made your list and arranged the items in their proper order, use it as a way of monitoring your life. Don't let any particular item on the list get way out of line in your everyday affairs. For instance, if you've decided that sex is not at the top of your list of pleasures, then don't let it usurp the number-one position in your daily life. Keep it in its place.

You can also use the list to monitor what doesn't give you pleasure. For instance, you may find yourself brooding compulsively about what happened to your marriage, or bad-mouthing your wife nonstop to all your friends. Check your list. Are brooding and bad-mouthing among your top ten pleasures? No, they're not. (Anyway, I hope not.) Then don't do them! They're in the category of things that give you momentary pleasure, like scratching a mosquito bite, but since they don't give true pleasure, they'll only make you more miserable in the long run.

If you've got a reasonably accurate picture of what does and what does not give you pleasure, you're that much ahead of the game—you'll be able to start steering yourself into activities that improve your mood and keep you from getting down in the dumps.

Focus Your Energies on Yourself

When you and your wife were still living together, you probably put a lot of effort and energy into your marriage. Now that the marriage has ended, that effort and energy have nowhere to go. This can be dangerous. That energy will come out *somehow,* one way or another. The danger is that it will come out in destructive ways, such as:

> trying to get revenge on your wife
> compulsively rehashing your marriage in your mind; living in the past
> becoming a workaholic
> becoming an alcoholic
> yelling at the children
> brooding all the time and getting depressed
> running around with lots of women; taking out your frustrations on them

The best way to avoid falling into this trap is to focus your unused energy on yourself. All the positive emotion you used to focus on your wife and your marriage, you can refocus on yourself.

How do you go about this? You can't do it if you're really emotionally upset. Try to calm down long enough to think rationally about your marriage. What were the good qualities you brought to the marriage, particularly the good emotional qualities? For instance, you may decide that you brought a lot to the marriage in the way of gentleness, patience, sensitivity, and caring. Or you may have been big on jolliness, good humor, tolerance, and a life-of-the-party spirit.

Now that you're single again, take these same qualities and apply them to yourself. If you're lucky enough to have these qualities, why not put them to good use?

For instance, if one of your particular qualities during your married days happened to be your gentleness, then be gentle with yourself now that you're single. Take things easy. You may find you've been dealing too harshly with yourself. Don't blame yourself needlessly for the breakup of the marriage. Don't kick yourself for having handled things badly. Don't take yourself to task for every little fault that comes up in your everyday life. Don't be needlessly harsh on yourself. Bury the past and build the present.

Or, if you were particularly tolerant in your marriage, then treat yourself to this quality now that you're single. Give yourself the same consideration you used to give your wife. Allow yourself some space to breathe. Don't try to force yourself into quick "fixes." Don't shoehorn yourself into a new relationship or remarriage before you're really ready. Give yourself a reasonable amount of time to recover from your separation. Don't rush things. You now have more time for yourself; use it.

This is really the single best way to put yourself into a better mental state during the early stage of your separation, because you're making use of your own best qualities. You're dealing from strength—you're using your real strong points where they can do the most good. You're not trying to force yourself to be someone you're not.

A Few Other Ways of Coping

Read a "positive" self-help book. Almost any book will do, whether it's specifically about marriage or not. It could be anything from *Pulling Your Own Strings* to *How to Win Friends and Influence People*. The important point is that it should have an underlying philosophy that says you have options to make your life better.

Go out for lunch. When you're depressed on the job or have a hard time getting through the day, force yourself to go out. It's simple but it helps. Focus on "beauty"—the waitress in the restaurant . . . the trees in the park . . . the boats on the lake.

Treat yourself. When you're having a bad attack of emotion, don't suffer in silence like a martyr. Do something nice for yourself. Frankly, the best thing is to spend money. (One thing every *woman* knows is that there's nothing like a good long shopping trip to make her feel on top of the world. Well, it works the same way for men.) Okay, I know you don't have money to throw around. Who does? But at least go to a movie, or drive to McDonald's and get a Big Mac, or go buy that pair of gloves you've promised yourself for the winter. This is only a Band-Aid, but it can help stop some of your emotional bleeding.

Call somebody. When you feel one or another emotion starting to get a little too heavy, you can often nip it in the bud by making a phone call and hearing a friendly voice. A positive, clearheaded friend is perfect, but anybody is better than nobody.

Don't let people lecture you. Some days it seems as if everybody likes to tell you when, how, and why your marriage went on the rocks. "You sure made a mess of things." "How could you abandon those beautiful kids?" "If you'd only listened to my advice a year ago, none of this would have happened." *Don't listen.* You need bucking up, not tearing down. Parents and other relatives, close friends, and sometimes co-workers are usually the worst offenders. Tell them bluntly that if they can't say anything positive, don't say anything at all.

Think ahead to when you'll see the kids next. This can be a lifeline. "They'll be here on Friday. If I can just get through these three days, I'll see them then and we'll have a wonderful time together."

Exercise. Physical action soothes mental stress. Any exercise will do, but a social exercise is even better than a solitary one, since you're playing with other people and won't feel so lonely. This puts racket games, dancercise, baseball, and the like ahead of jogging, swimming, or working out.

Cut down on sugar. Physiologically, sugar tends to make you hyperactive and jumpy. (It affects some people more than others.) You're upset enough without this added stimulus. Soothe yourself with carbohydrates like potatoes, bread, spaghetti, or rice.

Pay a lot of attention to how you look. Go on a diet; join an exercise class; grow a mustache; go to a really good hair-cutter; buy some new clothes. In the first place, this helps keep you occupied, gives you something to do—and activity is important to your mental equilibrium. Second, it helps your self-image: if you look better, you'll get better responses from people (especially women).

And last:

DON'T DRINK. You may think a drink will help, but it won't. Every separated father who has been through it says, "Lay off the booze." The same thing goes for drugs, in spades.

The Good Side of Separation

There *is* a good side, after all. It's not all bad. You'll feel better if you pay attention to what you're gaining rather than what you're losing. Don't scorn the corny old proverbs—Accentuate the positive, Every cloud has a silver lining, The night is darkest just before dawn. Write them out in capital letters and paste them on your desk, your bathroom mirror, your refrigerator door—where you'll be forced to stare at them every day.

And if you're in any doubt as to what the benefits of separation are, here's a list:

You don't need to compromise anymore. You're the sole boss in your house now. You can do things your way, without argument, criticism, or tension. You can have the car on Thursday night . . . you can have blue walls in the bedroom . . . you can eat TV dinners from the aluminum tray . . . you can throw out the leftovers . . . without having to go through endless discussions with someone else.

You'll have a one-on-one relationship with the kids. No conflicts with your wife will get in the way of your household activities. You'll probably be closer to the kids than when you were living with your wife. And when the kids are with you, there won't be any doubt that you are (for the time being) the most important adult—the *only* adult—in their lives.

Separation is better than a bad marriage. No matter how miserable you may (temporarily) feel, think of how much worse you'd feel if you were locked into your marriage with no prospect of getting out. The kids will probably feel better, too. Even if they have tantrums and depressions at first, they'll quickly sense—and be grateful for—the lessening of tension in their daily routine. They'll get more quality time now from both parents.

The kids will grow up more mature and experienced from having two households. They'll also be more responsible, from having to share more directly in the workings of each household.

You'll grow. If you haven't grown up yet—if you still have some mental and emotional baby fat around the edges—the divorce will sweat it out of you. I suppose you could actually say that most divorces are caused because the spouses got married before they were really grown-up. Now, if you play your cards right, you can use the divorce as a spur to give you a boot up the ladder of maturity.

You're in good company. It seems as if everybody gets divorced these days. It's not like getting cancer or having a heart attack or going bankrupt or falling down and breaking your leg—those are solitary, rare occurrences. With divorce, you're never alone. So when you walk down the street and see all the happy couples (gritting your teeth because you're single and miserable), just say to yourself, "Half of them will be divorced in a few years, just like me."

To end on a note of farce . . . when you worry about not having enough money, just remember what a wisecracking friend told me in the same situation: "Hell, just think how much money you'll save on toilet paper now that there's not a woman in the house."

3.

RECREATING YOUR FAMILY

Your Children Are Your Family

The real reason separated fathers are often miserable is that they have a deep-down, gut-level feeling that they've lost their families. They've lost that whole comforting support system known as The Family—Mom and Dad and the children and a house and a car and a dog—that classic, corny, American-as-apple-pie family.

Not so corny, really. If it were corny, we wouldn't all be in love with the idea. We wouldn't all hate to see our wonderful, mind's-eye existence blown to hell.

Example: When I was married, I got a lot of comfort and pleasure out of being part of a family. I particularly remember one day when it all stood out clear as air. My wife and I had taken our son to visit my parents. Just a regular Sunday outing. Nothing extraordinary about it, but as we walked away from my parents' house after the visit, all the elements fell suddenly into place. There we were, my wife and I, with our son between us, holding his hands. On the porch were my parents, waving good-bye to us and beaming with pride at having this classic image of a happy family. Ahead of us was our own house, our own cozy nest. The picture included everything but a faithful dog running at our heels (and a few months later we had that, too).

Well, the whole scene stuck in my mind like a snapshot, absolutely indelible. When, several years later, Linda and I separated, this scene would come back to haunt me. It seemed to crystallize everything I was losing through separation. I couldn't keep it out of my mind, though every time I thought of it, I'd end up weak with regret and misery.

Something like this happens to most separated fathers. Whether we admit it or not, we have an image in the back of our minds of the ideal family. It may be corny, it may be unrealistic, but it sure as hell is potent. And so when the image is violated—by separation or divorce—we feel an awful lot of pain and disappointment, plus a very unpleasant sense of failure.

If divorce were only a matter of getting rid of a spouse, unhappy couples wouldn't wait two seconds before heading for the courtroom. But of course the spouse is only a small part of it. The real trauma of divorce comes not from losing a wife but from losing a family.

And here's where our idealized images of family life really throw us for a loop. We have this image in our mind's eye—for most of us, it's the only image of family life we've ever had, or even thought of. Nothing else has occurred to us. So when the divorce comes along, that image is shot to pieces, a pretty picture reduced to incoherent fragments.

If only we didn't have that one and only picture of family life lodged so firmly in our minds. But most of us were weaned on it, and by now it's part of our psyches. But if only we had a somewhat broader or less specific idea of family life, then we wouldn't be so traumatized by divorce. Divorce absolutely kills our classic definition of the family, but it wouldn't necessarily kill another definition.

There's no law that says an ideal family has to have two adults living in the same house, no law that says you can't have a family if you don't have a wife. So if you're hung up on the idea that you've lost your "family," just keep telling yourself you haven't. I've seen the basic idea expressed in several ways, all of which make the point succinctly and truly (like mottoes embroidered on samplers):

"Just because you've lost your wife doesn't mean you've lost your family."

"You're an ex-husband, not an ex-father."

"Your children are your family."

Once you get to the point of accepting these notions on a gut level, you've conquered many of the troublesome emotions of separation.

Actually there are advantages to the single-parent family. This is not just hyperbole. Sometimes when I mention this idea to people, I can see that they think I'm just talking, just trying to make the best of a bad lot. It's obvious they believe that a two-parent family is the real thing and a single-parent family nothing but a poor imitation.

Not true. Thinking that a single-parent family is just a smudged copy of a two-parent family is part and parcel of the hammerlock that traditional thinking has on people. I'm not saying that you'd necessarily *choose* single parenthood if you had the choice—just that it does have real pluses.

• There's less tension. The constant undercurrent of strife between Mom and Dad is gone. There will still be some tension, of course, among family members—that's inevitable in any kind of family—but the tangle of mismatched emotions that characterizes a rocky marriage will be gone.

• The family is more democratic. Dad has a more one-on-one relationship with the children; the children have more say in family decisions and planning. You may not necessarily think this is a good thing—especially if you're the type who likes to rule the roost with an iron hand—but it's actually a gift in disguise, since it gives you the opportunity for a closer relationship with your children.

• There's more flexibility in planning your life with the children. There's only you and them to consider, not Mom anymore. Mom plans her life with the children separately. Everybody is happier all around.

• You become more mature. In a two-parent family, each spouse often tries to conceal some of the other spouse's more unattractive qualities from the children. In a single-parent family, you don't have another adult to cover for you, so all your failings are much more obvious to the children. This can be a powerful incentive to clean up your act.

• They're more responsible. They have to take responsibility for helping around the house, since neither parent now can do all the work alone. They also have to cope with a certain amount of responsibility for facing and conquering the emotions of the divorce. Kids from single-parent homes often seem much more competent, less sheltered and helpless than other children of the same age who are living with two parents.

• They're more independent. Children in a two-parent home sometimes develop too much dependence on the family. It's "the family against the world" for them, and they may be rather hesitant to venture outside the familiar bounds of the family. When children are dealing with two parents in separate homes, however, they are prevented from developing too great a dependence on either one. They begin to see, for instance, that everyone has to stand on his own two feet, and that they can't hide behind Mom and Dad.

• They're more tolerant. Children in two-parent families tend to see only one version of life and the world: the version presented by their family. As a result, they may not develop the perception that other people and other parts of life may be very different from their own little corner of the world. Children in one-parent families, on the other hand, have more than one perspective on the world; hence they have a more realistic, three-dimensional picture of how things really are. This makes them more tolerant of other people, of change, and of things that are different from their narrow experience of life.

• They're more emotionally mature. They're exposed to two different emotional styles: Mom's and Dad's. In two-parent houses, parents tend to present a united front to the children, and so their emotional differences often get muted. But if the parents are living apart, the children have to learn to adapt to two very different human beings.

Children's Reactions to Separation and Divorce

The first thing you'll have to deal with as a single father is your children's emotional reaction to your separation. One thing you can say with 100 percent accuracy about your separation is:

THE KIDS WON'T LIKE IT

Separation means change, and children don't like change. They don't like upsets in their established ways of doing things. Separation is one of the biggest upsets possible to imagine, so you can be sure they're going to have pretty strong reactions. Even if they are basically relieved that you and their mother have split and that there won't be the same tension in the air anymore, they'll still be annoyed and disturbed by the ensuing changes in their daily routines and living conditions.

Having said that, I should also say:

JUST BECAUSE KIDS DON'T LIKE IT DOESN'T MEAN IT'S BAD

Kids may not like wearing sweaters to school . . . putting on rubbers on rainy days . . . washing their hands before meals . . . or spinach. But this isn't to say that these things are bad. It's the same with separation. Children will hate the idea of your splitting up, but that in itself is no reason to avoid or put off the separation. And by the same token, it's no reason to stick it out with your wife if both of you know you'd be better off divorced.

Very young children and babies may not be very vocal about a separation between Mom and Dad. They won't completely understand what's going and in any case won't be able to verbalize their feelings completely. Kids between the ages of three and ten will kick and scream at the idea, just as they throw tantrums at any development they don't like. Kids over ten, especially teenagers, may act very cool about the separation. "Oh, you and Mom are getting separated? So what?" But underneath it all, every child, no matter what his age, will be thrown for a loop by his parents' separation. Whether he expresses his feelings or not, the feelings are certainly there. And they'll come out in certain kinds of behavior and displays of emotion.

This is what the new single father has to be on the watch for. Children will have an easier time getting over the hump of separation if their parents are able to lend them a helping hand. This isn't easy for the parents, since (in most cases) they've never been through a separation before and they don't know what to be on the lookout for in their children. It's a brand new situation for which Mom and Dad haven't had any advance preparation or education.

When you're in this situation, you'll make plenty of wrong moves with your children. This is inevitable, since there's no such thing as a perfect parent. But this doesn't mean you should take your mistakes lightly or forget about trying to improve yourself as a parent. All of us at one time or another screw up parts of our children's lives because we're ignorant of how to guide them through periods of heavy weather. The more we can learn about dealing with our children, the better.

USEFUL FACT: Children, from toddlers to teens, have pretty standard reactions to separation. It's not as though the single father is going to be faced with behavior that has never been seen before on the face of the earth. If he is suddenly faced with odd and unusual behavior from his children, he can rest assured that someone—in fact, many fathers—has faced just this same behavior many times before.

Since forewarned is forearmed, here's a rundown—as complete as I can make it—of the reactions you're likely to see in your children.

Denial. The easiest way for a child to avoid the consequences of a hateful situation is simply to deny that the situation is happening. You may tell your young son or daughter that you and Mom are going to live in separate houses from now on, but if that's not what he or she wants to hear, he or she may let it go in one ear and out the other and persist in believing that the separation is only temporary, like a vacation or a business trip. The child won't be angry, won't be hurt, won't cry, won't throw tantrums—will just be silent. The situation shouldn't be allowed to go on too long; sooner or later, the strain of denying reality gets too strong for the child, and neurotic problems begin to poke up their heads.

Usually the best way to deal with the situation is to force the child to face reality—but in such a way that reality is not so terrifying as he had feared. *Show* him; don't *tell* him. The passage of time will go a long way toward alleviating the problem. Meanwhile, don't lecture him with a lot of words; instead, show him your new apartment (or wherever you're living) as soon as possible. Let him see with his own two eyes that you now have a place of your own. The more contact the child has with your separate existence, the better. Don't visit him at Mom's place. Bring him to your place, even if only for a few hours. Take him to visit your office . . . invite him to go shopping with you . . . let him stay overnight with you at your place, if he wants to. And don't let him wheedle or cajole you and Mom into having dinner together with him or jointly tucking him into bed "just this once."

Anger. Children are often angry at situations they can't control. It's their standard reaction. If your children are angry, it's par for the course. (You should be more surprised if they're *not* angry.) Their anger is usually of the "I hate you" sort. "I hate you—you moved out and left me." "I hate you—you made Mommy leave." "I hate you—you're hurting me." The temptation is to yell right back. Don't. It's not their fault they're angry . . . not their fault the separation is occurring. And though it seems as if they're attacking *you*, they're not really; they're not angry with you so much as they're angry with the situation. It's just that you happen to be the easiest person to vent the anger on, so you get the "I hate you" routine.

Don't take it personally. Let them yell and get it out of their systems. Just say, "Boy, are you angry," and let them go on yelling. They'll wind down eventually and be all the better for the outburst. They may have flare-ups of anger for years, literally. You'll just have to live with it. It's vital for them to discharge their feelings. (One reason so many adults are hurting is because they weren't allowed to discharge their feelings as children; they were forced to be "adult" too soon and to keep their emotions inside.) When dealing with your children, a point to remember is that you're not dealing with a child who has to be corrected—you're dealing with a person who has to be brought out. And the way to do this is simply to listen, even if you're forced to listen to a lot of stuff you don't want to hear.

Children often express their anger by fighting among themselves. This may be their way of trying to get and hold your attention. One way to deal with this is to let them have enough of your attention in other ways so that they don't have to seek it through fighting. When they do start shouting, tune out. If you pay attention, they'll only do it more. Let them fight it out. Or just say, "If you want to fight, go outside and do it. I don't mind your fighting, but the noise is disturbing me."

"Is it my fault?" Children almost always struggle with this question. They wonder if *they* have caused the separation. Children, especially ones under ten, see themselves as the center of the universe, and it often appears to them that they are the cause of situations that in reality have nothing to do with them. Even confident, outgoing children—even teenagers—will wonder if Mom and Dad are getting a divorce because of them. "Maybe they're tired of me." "Maybe they're getting a divorce because I kept spilling my milk." "If I'd been better, maybe they wouldn't have split up." From their perspective, it appears that the divorce is your way of punishing them for something they've done.

This is an irrational fear, so it does no good for you to attack it with cold logic. A warm hug is the best way to reassure a child that it's not his fault—a warm hug and some reassuring words. "It's not your fault. I know sometimes we've gotten mad at each other, but that doesn't have anything to do with it. I'll always love you." And keep on saying this. Children's fears don't go away immediately; they keep cropping up. You may think you're starting to sound like a broken record, constantly reassuring the child, but he won't think so; he'll appreciate it.

You can also be on the alert for expressions of the children's imaginary guilt, for this is the best time to buck them up with reassurances.

"Are you divorcing me, too?" Young children who don't grasp the concept of divorce often get hung up on this question. They get the idea that divorce means you are divorcing the whole family.

Reassure them. "Divorce can only happen between grown-ups.

It doesn't affect you and me. You'll always be my daughter, and I'll always be your father. There's no way I can divorce you, and there's no way you can divorce me. We'll always have each other."

Divorce as crime. Children often associate lawyers and courts with crime. Since you and your wife are dealing with lawyers and going to court, the children may assume you've committed a crime. Or they may assume that one of you must be the "good guy" and the other the "bad guy." Since it's usually you, the father, who is cast in the role of the bad guy, this misapprehension shouldn't be allowed to remain in the children's minds.

Some elementary explanations are in order. "This is a different kind of courtroom from what you see on TV. Nobody's on trial. It's not a matter of crime. The judge is just helping us make a decision —he's not the same kind of judge who bangs a gavel and says 'Guilty!' Your mother and I need the judge because we're having a hard time making the decision ourselves. The judge will help us decide, and he'll also sign the papers that make it all legal."

The calmer you are, the calmer your children will be. Children pick up on your own fears and apprehensions, and if you're fearful about what will happen now that you're going to court, the children will be, too.

Hope for reunion. Unless the state of affairs in the household before the separation was really intolerable, almost all children will harbor the fantasy or the hope that their parents will patch up their differences and get back together again. Even if Mom and Dad fought like wild animals and yelled at the children more than they deserved, the children, through force of habit if nothing else, will still usually half-expect or half-hope that the separation will evaporate and the family will go back to its old self.

Children usually get over this idea relatively easily when they see that the parents are serious about staying apart. The operative word here is *serious*. The parents shouldn't hold out false hopes to the children about a reunion. And they shouldn't put on a sweet, lovey-dovey act for the children whenever they meet each other. The strongest way to get the message across to the children is to show them that two complete homes now exist, one for each parent. If both Mom and Dad have a place of their own—a real

home, not just a motel room or some other place to park their bags
—then the children will get the idea—more forcefully than if you
put it into words—that the split between the parents is permanent.

Divorce as a contest. If the parents squabble over the divorce
settlement—"I'll give you the car if you'll let me have the house
for the next two months"—the children may get the idea that the
divorce is a sort of contest in which the two contestants (Mom and
Dad) collect the prizes. Actually, in some cases, this may be pretty
close to the truth. The only problem is that the children often
come to see themselves as one of the prizes—"You can have the
children every weekend if you'll agree to raise the alimony pay-
ment." Naturally, the children feel dehumanized by this. They
may assume that they're unloved, since they're being treated as
items in a bargaining contest.

The best way to sidestep this problem is to avoid discussing the
divorce settlement in front of the children or even making statements like, "If you want custody of the children, then you'd better
start being a little more conciliatory . . ." If they don't know you
and your wife are haggling over custody or property settlements,
they won't get the idea that you're involved in a contest, and they
won't feel like pawns in the game.

Loss of love. When one parent moves out, the children wonder,
"Doesn't he (or she) love me anymore? Is he leaving because he
has stopped loving me?" The question often doubles for other
questions that the child doesn't put into words, such as, "Why
don't you pay attention to me anymore?" or "Why are you always
ignoring me and worrying about other things?"

The child's apprehensions are sometimes quieted by telling him
bluntly, whenever the question arises, "Yes, I still love you and I'll
always love you," and by paying him routine attention so that he
doesn't feel he's being forgotten. Regular visits to the children—or
regular trips on their part to visit you—are the best way to maintain a "presence" in their lives and prevent their worrying about
losing your love.

Even when you're mad, or feeling lousy, don't take out your
discontent on the children. This will only fuel their worry. You

may feel like saying, "Let the children put themselves out for me once in a while. With them, it's all take and no give. I'm the one who really needs help." You may need help, but if so, you'll have to get it elsewhere—not from the children. You're the adult, and it's up to you not to burden them with responsibility they're not equipped to bear.

"Will mom leave, too?" When Dad leaves, it's only natural for the children to wonder if Mom will leave, too. The child basically fears being abandoned, being left on his own with no one to care for him.

This question usually arises in children's minds when the father moves out and is erratic in visiting them (or having them visit him). If he maintains a regular schedule with the children, then the idea that he has left or abandoned them won't be so strong, and they'll have no impetus to frame the next question: "Will Mom leave us, too?"

"Where will I live?" When children see the household being split up, they may get nervous about whether they'll have a permanent place to live. The underlying question they're worried about is this: "Will I have a home at all—or will I be left out in the cold?"

Children are reassured by specifics. Therefore, if they ask this question, answer them as specifically as possible. "You'll live with Mommy during the week and with me on Saturday and Sunday." Then add a few reassuring generalities to answer the unspoken questions. "There will always be a place for you to live. Your mother and I will always make sure you have a home."

Can I keep the dog? my new guitar? the goldfish? During the period of separation or divorce, children have a generalized sense of loss. They may feel that since they are "losing" one parent, they may also lose other things that are important to them. This can be profoundly disturbing to them. The first thing they think of is pets, but any other valued possession or privilege may be involved.

A simple reassurance is usually enough. "Of course you can keep the canaries." If, however, they cannot keep the desired object— say they want the dog and you're taking the dog with you—then soften the blow as much as you can. "The dog will come to live with me on Elm Street. You'll see him every weekend when you're with me. Let's go over there tomorrow to find the best place for his bed."

In answering any of the questions children have about the separation, or in quieting the fears they express, it helps to bear in mind that children need three things to maintain a state of healthy equilibrium: routine, continuity, and specifics. The more you can do to bolster their supply of these three qualities, the happier they'll be—and the less likely they'll be to have the adverse reactions I've listed here.

Routine: a sense that basic activities and surroundings are comfortably familiar and are not constantly being changed.

Continuity: a sense of stability from day to day, a sense that next week can be depended on to be not too different from this week. Continuity can be fostered by letting children know what to expect next week, next month, next year; by making plans and sticking to them; by not changing horses in midstream.

Specifics: having things concrete, cut and dried, not vague or conditional. Saying "I'll see you Sunday," rather than "I'll see you soon." Specifics can be fostered by being clear, to the point, and, especially, honest—not evading children's questions or fudging your responses.

How Not to Damage the Children

Children are usually more resilient than parents expect. Given half a chance, they bounce back from the upsets of separation or divorce and are none the worse for the experience. It's only when things get hairy during a particularly difficult separation that children are likely to suffer any really damaging scars.

Not that the separating parents intend to do any damage to their children. That's not it. It's just that the children happen to get caught in a situation the intensity or danger of which the parents don't quite comprehend, and so they get hurt unintentionally.

I'd say that in eight out of ten divorces, the children come out of the experience pretty well. In the other two, they get banged up and need a couple of years, sometimes, to recover. But always, even in the relatively amicable divorces, I see at least a few little painful traps that the children unwarily stumble into—or are pushed into. Inevitably the parents don't realize they have been setting the traps for the children—and if somebody actually points this out to them, they are open-mouthed with surprise. "My God, I had no idea I was giving the children *that* idea." "But I had no intention of hurting the children." "How on earth could the children have possibly thought that was what I meant?" "It never occurred to me that my actions could be seen in that light." Et cetera.

The most common situation is one in which the children get caught in a crossfire between the two sniping parents. But other situations occur that involve only one parent—usually a situation in which the parent (either the father or the mother) makes unfair or overtaxing demands on the children, not realizing that he or she is doing so.

A Few No-nos

Bad-mouthing their mother. Sure, you're at your wit's end with her—sometimes she really has you climbing the wall—but that's your affair; it's not the children's affair. It's easy to blow off steam to them. After all, they're *there;* they are a captive audience for you to shout at. "I swear, your mother has no idea of the value of money!" "She's the most disorganized woman I've ever met." "Lies, lies, lies. That's all I get from her." "I don't know how you children'll ever put up with living alone with your mother." "All she thinks about is money."

Even if you really have nothing against your ex-wife, you can still find yourself expressing anger to the children. This happened to me a lot following my own separation. I missed my wife and my marriage, and it was so much easier to be angry about it than to be sad. Unfortunately, it was my son who had to bear the brunt of it.

Even if your wife is the most heartless, incompetent, mercenary, dishonest woman in the world, she's still the children's mother and they love her. More to the point, they're going to have to live with her (at least part of the time). Your bad-mouthing her in front of them will only confuse and annoy them and make their relationship with her more difficult. Also—and this may be the crux of the matter—bad-mouthing your wife won't make the children love *you* any more (although this is what you may secretly want). The mud you sling at her simply won't stick.

Forcing the children to "choose." This doesn't usually happen in its pure form: "Okay, children, choose between your mother and me —you can't have both of us." But it can take plenty of watered-down forms that still manage to put the children in a very unpleasant position. No child wants to have to choose one parent over the other; the child wants both parents. Anything that forces him into the position of having to make a choice is unnatural and unfair. "If you stay with your mother this weekend, forget about coming on vacation with me in the summer." "I bet you'd rather be with me than with Mommy, wouldn't you, sweetheart?" "If you want me to come and watch you in the baseball game, then don't ask your mother, too!"

Egging on the children to anger against Mom. Children have bouts of anger against both parents before, during, and after a divorce. It's a way of letting off steam. Naturally you'll hate it when their anger is aimed at you—but you may have a sneaking (or not so sneaking) feeling of pleasure when their anger is aimed at their mother. It's tempting to throw a few coals on the fire of their anger. "She sure *is* mean, isn't she?" "You have every right to hate her." "My God, I can understand your being angry at her—she makes me angry all the time, too." The children's anger against Mom is their affair, not yours. When they sound off against her in your presence, let them talk—but don't join in.

Leaving decisions up to them. Children aren't old enough to make major decisions, so they shouldn't have decisions forced on them. "Your mother and I just don't know what to do. We've decided that we'll get back together again if you children really want us to." Not in a million years should such a decision be thrust onto the children. *Of course* they want you to get back together—and they'll say so—but they'll feel that the decision isn't what you wanted to hear, and they'll be awfully uncomfortable about it. Another example of forcing unfair decisions on the children:

"Would you rather live with your mother or me? We'll do whatever you prefer." Adult decisions should be made by adults. To ask the children to make such decisions is to put them in a no-win situation: whatever they decide, they've displeased one or both of their parents.

Threatening children with abandonment. This can take either the blunt form—"Honestly, you children drive me crazy. I'd like to just go off and leave you behind"—or the subtle form—"I know you didn't mean it, darling, but it upset Daddy anyway, and now Daddy has to go away for a rest." Or it can be a threat: "Pick up your room this minute or you can go right back to your mother!" No matter how rhetorical your statements may be—you may not really mean it—the children, literal-minded as they are, may immediately take the statement to its logical conclusion and wonder, "Is he going to abandon me forever?" Even if you're angry and lose your head, don't threaten the children with abandonment. Of all the things you can say to children, this is the most poisonous—it can throw a pall over your new family relationship for months or years.

Comparing the children to their mother. This rarely happens except in anger. "You are just like your mother—whining all the time." "Stop that! Your mother always does that, and it drives me crazy." "I can see you got your frivolity from your mother." This is a variation on the theme of bad-mouthing your wife, except that you're bad-mouthing both your wife and your child at the same time, which is worse.

The Three Overs

It's also possible to go too far in the opposite direction—to kill the children with kindness, so to speak. Far from being angry or unpleasant with them, you're too nice. This is where we run into the three *overs:* overnurturing, overindulgence, and overreacting.

When children stop having one home and start having two, they get a double dose of parenting. Both parents may be going overboard to "be both father and mother to the children." It's as though the children suddenly have two mothers and two fathers. They may think they're seeing double. This kind of overparenting can reach almost comical proportions when both Mom and Dad are competing for the title of Best Possible Parent. The children find themselves swamped with affection, attention, and solicitude until they may almost want to shout, "Oh, why don't you just leave us alone for a minute!" More insidious, they may luxuriate in the overnurturing like fat cats in a nest of pillows—to the point that they fail to develop an ability to cope with life on their own.

Overindulgence is akin to the doting grandparent syndrome—smothering the children with gifts, presents, and indulgence in what is basically an attempt to buy affection. It may also develop from a sense of guilt: "I hurt the children when I separated from their mother, so now I have to make it up to them by being especially nice." And then again, part of it may be due to plain old-fashioned fear: "If I'm not extraindulgent of the children, they may want to spend all their time with their mother and not see me at all." But overindulgence is never good, *especially* when both parents are competing at it; it leads to dependent children who have an unattractively cynical attitude toward their parents.

Overreacting happens all the time to conscientious parents who feel guilty or apprehensive about the separation's effect on the children. It's as though the minute they separate, they forget everything they've learned about being a parent and start behaving like greenhorns with a newborn baby. "Oh my God, she's crying. Quick. Do something!" "What's wrong with him? Why is he acting that way?" "Oooops! What have I done? I've done something awful to her! Help!"

Overreacting won't help your state of mind, and it may drive the children crazy. ("Oh, for heaven's sake, Dad, calm down, will you?")

There's a good old-fashioned cure for the three *overs:* be yourself. Just because you're separated doesn't mean you're a different person. And it doesn't mean the children are different people, either. There's no need to change your style; you don't suddenly have to start overnurturing them, overindulging them, overreacting to them. The children will expect you to stay the way you were. They'll be surprised and bewildered if you turn into a strange fairy godfather who hovers over them with affection, smothers them with attention, and has an anxiety attack whenever they do anything in the least bit unusual.

Keeping Yourself in Line: Questions to Ask Yourself

- Do I ever threaten to leave the children if they don't do what I tell them?
- Do I ever dump on their mother in their presence?
- Do I ever give them the impression that I'm mad or displeased when they say they love Mommy?
- Do I ever encourage the children to be angry at their mother?
- Am I happy when the children get angry at Mom?
- Do I argue with my ex-wife when the children are present?
- Do I moan to the children about how miserable I feel?
- Do I let the children get away with behavior I wouldn't have tolerated before my separation?
- Am I trying to prove I'm a better parent than my ex?
- Do I tell the children about my financial problems? personal problems? emotional problems? legal problems?
- Do I give the children lots more gifts and presents than I did before the separation?

Kids + Dad = Family

Once you've separated, you'll start getting used to a new definition of *family*. From now on, it's you and the children. Just because this is a different kind of family from the one you're used to having doesn't mean it's any less valid. Guys who are hung up on traditional definitions are the same ones who feel panicky because they're "losing their children" or "no longer have a family" or "feel so alone in the world." If they'd throw away the old, standard definition of *family*, they'd be a lot less worried about their future. As long as they keep in touch with their children at all, they have a family.

The delicate part of the whole operation is finding the right new equilibrium for your new family. The old equation was Mom + Dad + Kids = Family. Now that Mom has been subtracted from the equation, the other elements—that is, Dad and the children—have to be rebalanced so that the family again finds a workable and harmonious equilibrium. (Incidentally, Mom is faced with the same problem; she has to find a new equilibrium in *her* relationship with the children.)

In rebalancing the family equation, it's inevitable that your relationship with your children will change. It *has* to change if the equation is to have any sort of stable and lasting balance. And the one basic change that affects all single fathers regardless of their individual situations, their custody arrangements, their personalities and those of their children is this: the father's role becomes that of an all-purpose parent rather than that of a traditional, narrowly defined "Dad."

It's not exactly that you're trying to be both a mother and a father to your children—that's an impossible task, no matter how many people try to accomplish it. I know, since I tried. The very same day my wife moved out, I told myself that nothing was going to change in the house. I'd be both parents to my son. Well, I only lasted three days at this. Then I broke down completely and had to admit I was trying to accomplish the impossible.

Once you're separated, you're no longer the Dad-half of a Mom-and-Dad duo. Your functions in the family no longer fit into that tidy little definition. Both you and your wife have to reposition yourselves, so to speak, so that you can cope with the children without having another person at your side.

Your relationship with your children is now strictly one-on-one. When you were still part of a Mom-and-Dad team, your relationship with each child was two-on-one. You didn't have an *individual* relationship with the children; you and their mother were always part of a pair. That's all changed now. And your relationship with your children, for better or worse, is definitely an *individual* relationship.

This leads to a big change in what the experts like to call the authority structure of the family. Back in the days when there were two of you in the relationship with each child, each of the kids had a sense, to be blunt about it, that he or she was outnumbered. Not that your relationship with your children was based on brute strength or force of numbers—just that each child had a healthy sense that the authority in the family was inevitably weighted in favor of the parents, who represented a higher echelon.

With a single parent, the force of numbers is lost, and inevitably your style of dealing with your children has to change. You can't prevail over the children by sheer force of numbers. The new one-on-one relationship means that your children will see you now more as an individual rather than as a member of a team. This implies that your relationship will in turn be more egalitarian and less authoritarian.

It's the old parent-vs.-pal situation. Your children won't view you in the old way simply as Dad. So which are you going to be—a parent or a pal?

Actually, you're going to be somewhere in between. You're not going to be simply a traditional Dad anymore, but neither (I hope) are you going to be just another buddy for the children to play with. No single father can sustain either the Dad role or the pal role for long. It just doesn't work. If a single father tries to act exactly as he used to act when he was still with his wife—without making any adjustments—he'll have a rebellion on his hands from the children and he'll also find himself faced with a ton of situations he's never had to face before. And if he goes overboard in the opposite direction and becomes a chum, the children will run wild and get into all sorts of problems because he's not giving them enough guidance.

In my own case, I went through a phase of trying to be my son's best friend. It didn't last long, thank heaven. I hadn't realized what a fool I was making of myself until my son told me that I was embarrassing him by acting that way in front of other people. He didn't know any other fathers who acted so chummy with their children, and he asked me bluntly to be more serious.

Sooner or later, any single father gets shivvied into a workable arrangement that's somewhere in between being a Dad and a pal. He becomes a person who can not only make rules for the children, lay down the law about household behavior, and administer punishment when punishment is deserved, but can also talk frankly to the children in a person-to-person manner, be honest and open about both his feelings and their feelings, and consult them as individuals and equals when family business is at stake.

It's not just the authority structure that has changed; *everything* has changed, such as:

Discipline: You no longer have a wife-in-residence to share discipline and to back you up in your disciplinary decisions. You've got to do it all yourself. On the other hand, you've also got to coordinate your style of discipline with your ex-wife so that neither of you undoes the other's work behind the other's back (if possible).

Money: Unless you're rich, money is in short supply. This affects your job, your home life, and the nitty-gritty of daily existence. You'll have to make adjustments in household expenditures, allowances, trips, vacations, and so on, and this in turn may cause subtle changes in your relationship with your children.

Attitude toward children: They probably will become more individualized, more important to you, since they are not just *part* of your family, they *are* your family. Of necessity, they'll also probably take on more family responsibility, even if it's only helping with chores around the house.

Children's attitude to you: Children will come to see that they're your partners in the family (albeit junior partners) rather than strictly subordinates, as they were when they had both Dad and Mom to contend with. They will be more likely to open up to you and discuss their personal problems and concerns. On the minus side, children often try to become "surrogate spouses," to replace the missing parent. This can cause problems if you have a daughter. (More on this in Chapter 10.)

Easing into Your New Role

After your separation, you'll slide into a new relationship with your children, whether you like it or not. The only question is how easily and how successfully you'll accomplish the transition.

Fathers who botch the job (through inflexibility or plain ignorance) may end up with bratty, neurotic children or no children at all. Frankly, though, it's hard to make a complete mess of the transition from married life to life as a single father. Goodwill is half the battle; if you *want* to have a decent family life with your children, you're already halfway to achieving it. (It's like the old saying about success in business: if you want it badly enough, you'll get it.)

Beyond goodwill, though, there's still plenty of room for the application of intelligence and common sense. Going through a separation and a divorce is a little like negotiating a stretch of white-water rapids in a rubber raft. Chances are you won't actually overturn and drown, but on the other hand, you may have a pretty bumpy ride if you don't keep an eye on the water and wield a strong hand with the paddle.

Requirement number one: don't worry too much. Fretting with guilt or worrying about your possible inadequacy is needless. If you were an adequate parent when you were married, you'll be an adequate parent now that you're separated. "But," the worriers will say, "we don't know how to cook . . . we don't know how to take care of the children by ourselves . . . we don't know what to do with the children all day on the weekend . . . we don't know how to comfort children when they cry . . . we'll make a mess of being single fathers."

This is beside the point. You don't have to be superman to be a successful father to your children. Nobody's asking you to be Dad, Mom, Grandpa, Grandma, and the fairy godmother all rolled into one. You don't have to be all things to all people.

Which brings me to a realistic piece of advice that was first given to me years ago by an experienced single father and that I've since repeated umpteen times to other separated men: build on your strengths. In your new relationship with your children, concentrate on the things you're good at. If you have a passion for sports, try to make sports a big part of your activities with your children. If the children love the way you read stories, then make a point to read stories whenever they're with you. If you're a good cook, then make a big point of making special family meals, getting the children to help you, letting them do the shopping, and so on. The flip side of this coin is just as important: if you're not good at any particular activity, don't try to force yourself into it. If housekeeping isn't your strong suit, then let the house get a bit dirty. If you can't cook worth a damn, have pizza delivered or eat TV dinners. If zoos bore you, take the children to the movies on Sunday instead. Kids usually won't notice the omissions—the things you *don't* do—whereas they will remember the fun of doing the things you are good at.

The important thing to ask yourself is, "Is this what I'm comfortable with," not, "Is this what is expected of me?" or "What will people think of me?" It's *your* family—just you and the children—and you have to find your own balance. Your friends may say, "George's place is always such a mess," or "The children never get a home-cooked meal when they're with Herman," or "How on earth can Jerry stand to go running off to museums every weekend with his daughter?" But if you're happy with the situation, then it doesn't matter what other people say. (I go along with that old Chinese saying, Fugg it.)

Of course, your children must be reasonably happy with the situation, too. The important word here is *reasonably*. You're a family, and like all families, you'll have to make compromises. If the children don't like living in a dirty house, they'll just have to accept it in return for the fun things they do with you—or else they'll have to clean the house themselves. Actually, single fathers are more likely to bend over backward for the children—so far backward that they let the children's smallest whims dictate the way the family lives. But this defeats the purpose of being a father in the first place. Part of being a father lies in making decisions and (occasionally) laying down the law. An even more important part lies in simply letting the children know *who you are*. The children can't get a sense of who you are if you're always doing what *they* want to do—or what you think they want to do—and never what *you* want to do. You can't erase yourself and still be a successful father.

So if it's your style to let the housework slide or to eat TV dinners, so be it. Let the children know it. There's no law that says you have to slave with the vacuum cleaner or spend hours over a hot stove for them. At some point, of course, you may have to compromise. The children may like one "real" meal every weekend, and they may like a cleaner house than you do. Okay, then compromise: cook the meal, or hire a cleaning person. But at least the children have seen that you have an individual personality, that you are a real person, not just an all-purpose machine for running a household.

The next most important thing in creating a workable new relationship with your children is to be honest with them. It bolsters a child's confidence to be told the truth—and confidence is exactly what the child needs when his or her parents are setting up two single-parent families. Parents themselves instinctively try to shield their children from the "harsh truth" by telling little white lies or letting children make false assumptions about what's going on. (The most common thing is to let children keep hoping that you and your ex-wife will get back together again.) But the parents' instinct in this case is usually wrong: children don't need to be shielded from basic truths.

If you actually ask children who have grown up in single-parent families, they'll tell you that their parents could have been more honest with them. "We can handle almost anything," the chorus goes, "if Mom and Dad are up front about it."

Honesty gives the child solid ground to stand on. At the beginning of the separation, honesty consists of letting the child know that you and your wife won't be getting together again . . . that the child will have two homes . . . that both parents will continue to care for him. After the divorce, honesty will consist of telling (or showing) the children that you're getting serious about your girlfriend (so that you don't spring a remarriage on them, out of the blue) . . . that you're considering moving to another city . . . that you're going to a psychiatrist.

You can be honest without going into tedious or confusing explanations. The cardinal rule is to tell children all they need to know *but no more.* "Yes," you can say when they ask you about your girlfriend, "Kara and I like each other very much," but you don't have to explain that you're sleeping with her or let them see you in bed together. "Yes, I'm going to a psychiatrist. He's trained to help people find out more about themselves," rather than, "Daddy's so miserable, sweetheart, he's afraid he's going to have a nervous breakdown."

As the lawyers say, stick to the facts.

A sidelight on honesty is that it's often good for *you* as well as for the children. If you're making a point of being truthful with them, some of it will rub off on you, and you may find yourself starting to be more truthful with yourself. This is what happened to me after my own separation. Lack of honesty had been one of the big problems that led to the breakup. I hadn't been able to be honest with myself and really examine my motives and feelings. After my separation, however, when I was forced to be honest with my son, for his sake, I also got more honest with myself. This was a bit painful, but it certainly did me a lot of good—it forcibly put me on the road to making a lot of changes in myself.

And it wasn't all bad: it gave me an honest look at my good points, too, and that was always an ego booster.

You Are What You Say

When you separate from your wife, you may not notice it, but a lot of words fade out of your everyday vocabulary, words like *family, wife,* and *home.* You don't use these words so often anymore because you no longer *have* a wife, a home, a family (or so you think). In their place, you start using words like *ex-wife, breakup, custody,* and *broken home.* It's a whole new vocabulary —we might call it the Divorce Vocabulary.

There's nothing surprising in all this—new situations breed new vocabularies—but there *is* a problem: the new words and phrases have built-in negative connotations that may affect your mental attitude without you even realizing it.

When you use terms like these in your conversation, or hear them from your friends, it can't help but make a dent in your self-confidence. The Divorce Vocabulary emphasizes negative concepts—failure, breakup, separation, loss—and so it puts you in a negative frame of mind.

The worst offenders are the legalistic terms like *custody* and *visitation,* which substitute bleak statutory lingo for flesh-and-blood reality.

Take *visitation rights.* Everybody uses the phrase without giving the words a second thought. Everybody is familiar with what they mean. If your wife has custody of the children and you see them on weekends, then you have visitation rights. That's what the divorce settlement says; that's what the court decreed; those are the words printed in black and white on the separation agreement. The phrase figures in at least three-fourths of all divorce settlements.

But, when you actually think about it, does it really, truthfully describe your situation? Do you really only *visit* your children? Do they only visit you? When you start to think about this, you'll see how inaccurate it is. "Dammit," you say, "I really love my children, and the time I spend with them is a lot more than mere *visiting.* I'm *living* with them. They're living with me."

I've known single fathers who've told me their whole mental state changed when they stopped using words like *visit* and *visitation.* They saw things in a new light. They didn't feel so cut off from their children, so disenfranchised as fathers. Once they got rid of the official idea that their children were merely visiting them and accepted the idea that their kids were actually living with them (even if it was only for a weekend at a time), they suddenly felt they were real fathers again, with real families.

The truth is, the official terminology—the words we hear every day—carries hidden biases that warp and distort the father's position. There's only one logical thing to do: stop using the official vocabulary.

You are what you say. If you stop using negative expressions and substitute positive ones, you'll start *being* less negative and more positive.

Instead of These:
"Yes, I have children but they live with my ex-wife."
"The children visit me every other weekend."
"When my marriage broke up. . . ."
"My wife has custody and I have visitation rights."

Try These:
"Yes, I have a family."
"My children live with me every other weekend."
"When the marriage ended. . . ."
"The children live with me eight days each month and with their mother the rest of the time."

Another term that can be a nuisance in some situations is *ex-wife*. It's accurate, strictly speaking, but it emphasizes the negative side of things. It defines her in terms of what she isn't, not what she is. She may resent this, just as you may resent being known merely as Marsha's ex-husband. It's not a big deal, perhaps, but if you can find a better term, why not use it?

Instead of *ex-wife*, try *the children's mother*. This is more accurate—it defines her in terms of her present role (the mother of your children) rather than in terms of her past role (your wife). And it's less judgmental, less negative than *ex-wife*, and also more impersonal (which is desirable now that you're separated)—the term no longer links her to you.

Three Thorny Areas

Decision-making. Since your new family situation involves a more one-on-one relationship with your children, it follows that the children should have a say in making decisions that affect the whole family. If you're the democratic type, fine; you won't have any problem adjusting to this new state of affairs. If you tend to be a dictator, however, you'll have to loosen up a little: you no longer have the leverage to be a dictator, since you don't live with your children full-time.

The children should feel that they have some input without feeling that they are being burdened with problems beyond their grasp. In decision-sharing, my suggestion is: to each appropriate to his age. Thus, a five-year-old can be consulted on what to have for dinner on Saturday, where to go on Sunday afternoon, what kind of dog to get for a pet. Teenagers, on the other hand, can be involved in more serious questions, such as whether the family should move to a new house, whether Dad should accept the new job offer, whether the custody arrangement should be changed.

As for the children's own problems, Dad shouldn't be too eager to rush in and solve them for the children. If the children have disagreements among themselves, don't necessarily try to settle the disputes yourself; simply lay down rules for fighting. "No yelling in the living room. No hitting below the belt. Other than that, fight it out among yourselves." For more difficult disputes, Dad can call a family council to try to thrash out the problem. He acts as mediator while the children try to settle their differences; only as a last resort does Dad lay down the law.

Privacy. Privacy is usually in short supply in one-parent families. Dad's house or apartment is *never* big enough; the children rarely have a room of their own, and often they may have only a closet or a drawer to which they can claim exclusive ownership. Not only that, but there seems to be less mental and emotional privacy, too. The children are always coming to Dad with problems, or Dad is having problems of his own. Dad has his antennas out to monitor the children's emotional state, and of course the children are positive high-definition radar trackers of Dad's ups and downs. Dad is always curious about how the children live when they're not with him; and the children, for their part, have plenty of unanswered questions about Dad's girlfriends.

After a while, everybody gets to feeling they're living in a goldfish bowl. It's the children, though, who usually have the worst part of the bargain. At least Dad has several days a week alone, when the children are with Mom. But the children don't get any time alone at all. On the contrary, they probably get less time alone than when they were in a two-parent family. Now Mom and Dad may both be so concerned about providing adequate parenting to the children that they start breathing down the children's necks.

Both Dad and the children should have a time and a place to be alone. It may not necessarily be *enough,* but at least everybody should respect it.

The important thing about privacy is not that everybody have a lot of it but that everybody's bit of privacy be respected. If Dad doesn't want to be disturbed on Sunday morning until nine o'clock, then that should be a law in the household. If the daughter has been assigned specific ownership of the hall closet, then nobody (not even Dad) should go near it. If the son prefers not to be interrupted in the kitchen when he's cooking, then the rest of the family should stay away religiously.

Kids manipulating parents. Children have a genius for playing parents off against each other. "Why can't I stay up till eleven?

Mom lets me do it." "You're so mean. I wish I were back at Mom's." Children instantly sense when Mom and Dad are competing with each other, when they are uncertain about the children's affection—and they shamelessly exploit the competition for their own advantage. And if the two parents are in any way uncertain of the children's affection, the children mine the situation for all it's worth. In extreme situations, children start saying things like, "Oh, Dad, I love you best," or "Mom doesn't understand me," or "I get so bored when I'm with Mom," which an uncertain father may eat up. Unfortunately, the children are probably saying exactly the same things to Mom.

If you hear any of these lines from your children, beware. Children should not be encouraged to make any comparisons at all between you and their mom. When you hear these lines from your children, you can be pretty sure you're being manipulated. To let it go on is to foster lying as a way of life and to give the children a false sense that they can manipulate the whole world. Since they don't fully realize what they're doing, it makes no sense to yell at them for it. An honest admonition is enough: "What your mother lets you do is between you and her. Your behavior there has nothing to do with your behavior here. When you're with me, the standards of behavior are strictly between you and me."

Children don't create the situation; they exploit it. It's your sense of competition with your wife—or your insecurity about the children's love and affection—that they're picking up on and magnifying. If you can change your own behavior, the children's behavior will automatically change to follow suit. In that sense, the children's manipulation of you is an early warning signal that there are some kinks in your style that have to be attended to.

Ten Suggestions

- Be true to yourself.
- Be honest.
- Be specific with the children, not vague.
- Respect your children's privacy, and teach them to respect yours.

- Listen.
- Be there.
- Don't talk about your ex-wife to the children, but don't mind if they talk about her.
- Ask the children's opinions when making family decisions.
- Don't preach, yell, cut off, or be judgmental. Establish the standards that are important to you, and stick to them.
- Expect to fail often, and don't let it bother you.

RUNNING A HOME AS
A SINGLE FATHER

A single-parent home is not just a two-parent home with one adult subtracted from the picture. It's a different beast entirely. Any man who thinks that running a home on his own is just a matter of learning to scrape by with the housekeeping—that is, learning to do the things his wife used to do when he was still married—has a surprise coming. True, he'll have more responsibilities, more things to do—but running a single-parent home involves more than just adding to his repertoire of household skills. It also means making some basic readjustments in his conception of what a household is and how it should be run.

Often, the husband is in a better position than the wife when it comes to setting up a new home following separation. He at least realizes that he'll have to learn a few new tricks, even if it's only taking the laundry to the Laundromat and shopping for food at the supermarket. The wife, on the other hand, has always known how to perform the standard repertoire of household functions and may not realize that any other adjustments are required.

Running a home is a matter of much more than housekeeping—although housekeeping looms large, like a sinister threat, in the minds of many newly separated men. "How will I ever keep the house clean?" "I don't know a damn thing about shopping." "I'll be damned if I'm going to scrub floors and clean bathrooms." "What the hell am I going to do about meals? My wife always did the cooking."

But frankly, these are the easiest problems to solve in setting up a new household. They come under the heading of unavoidable nuisances—and like most other such things, they provide more annoyance than real difficulty. If you're one of the few men (few people, for that matter) who has a passion for cleaning, or shopping, or doing laundry, or cooking, consider yourself lucky. Housekeeping won't be quite such a nuisance to you as it is to others.

We might as well admit it: most men hate housekeeping. One book on the sociology of American couples put it bluntly: "Married men have such an intense averson to housework that the more they do of it, the less happy they are, the more they fight with their wives and the greater the chances of divorce." It's practically as bad with single fathers. They didn't like housekeeping when they were married. They don't like it now that they're separated.

If you're like the majority and think housekeeping is a bore, then there *are* ways to avoid most of it, or at least lessen the bite it takes out of your time (more on this later in the chapter).

Most of the real trials and tribulations—or, as one of my more optimistic friends puts it, the "adventures"—of setting up a single-parent household arise from the fact that we don't admit we're actually setting up a *household*. Weekend fathers—men who have "visitation rights" and only see their kids on weekends—are particularly prone to this. And since most of us at one time or another are weekend fathers, there's hardly a single father who avoids this snare. "Why should I worry about the problems of having a household?" the theory runs. "I only see my kids on weekends. I don't *have* a household."

That, of course, is just where he is wrong.

As long as you've got kids, you've got a family—and if you're going to have your kids with you at all, you're going to have a household. And that means you're going to have all the things that come with it. There's no getting around the fact. Not only are you going to have the regular tasks of cooking, cleaning, shopping, and such (you're going to have these even if you never see your kids at all), but you're going to have to attend to other considerations that specifically come from having a family: readjusting your schedule to take into account the fact that the kids are around, giving the children chores around the house, setting up house rules (spoken or unspoken) to regulate family behavior, and so on. All these are part of "running a house."

Two Smart Moves

Before worrying about house rules, children's responsibilities, cooking, cleaning, and all the rest of the ins and outs of running a house, though, there are two particular adjustments that every single father should make.

First, you should make sure you have important phone numbers handy when the children are with you: doctor, hospital, ambulance, police, poison control center. In the hurly-burly of moving out of one household and setting up another, you may forget this elementary safety measure. It's not just a matter of protecting the children in emergencies. It's also a matter of protecting yourself against being accused of negligence by the children's mother if anything should happen to the children when they're with you. If you always have important phone numbers handy and can respond to any emergency *immediately*, nobody can say that the kids are unsafe in your care.

Second, whenever the children are with you at your house, be very precise and reliable about your schedule. If you say you're going out for fifteen minutes, then don't stay out for half an hour. If you tell them you'll be home at eleven o'clock, then make sure you do get home at eleven o'clock. If you ask them to call you at home during the week, then be at home to take their call at whatever time you've agreed on.

Sticking to your schedule may not be a life-or-death matter (as in the case of having telephone numbers always handy), but it will have a more important effect on the day-in day-out functioning of your family. Basic fact: children like reliable schedules with no upsetting last-minute changes. It's part of their need for routine and continuity. If you tell them you're running out for cigarettes, they'll begin to get very worried if you're not home within fifteen minutes. All sorts of half-articulated fantasies will fly through their minds. "Something terrible has happened." "Daddy has run away and left me." "Daddy's never coming back." "Daddy lied to me." "Daddy's doing something he doesn't want me to know about."

"What will happen next time Daddy says he's only going to be out for fifteen minutes?" "Can I trust Daddy?"

I remember once leaving my son in my apartment while I went out to the supermarket for a container of milk and juice. The supermarket was only two blocks away, but it was a beautiful day and I took my time sauntering along the street. Then I did some impulse buying at the supermarket and arrived back at the apartment an hour later with twenty dollars' worth of groceries. When I got there, my son was hysterical. He'd called his mother and she was on her way over (having canceled an important appointment), fully expecting to find that I'd been run over by a truck, had had a heart attack in the supermarket, or suffered some other terrible fate. Chris was relieved to see me but also very upset and angry at me about the whole episode. It was a powerful example of how children's imaginations can get out of control and how innocent mistakes can turn into traumas.

You may have had some of these same problems when you were married, but in less severe form. Your wife was usually there to cover for you. "Daddy must have been held up in traffic. Don't worry. He'll be here soon." "Yes, I know Daddy said he'd call, but perhaps he's having trouble with the phone." Now there's no one to smooth over your omissions and quiet the children's fears when you don't perform as you said you would.

The firmer your schedule, the better. If you can't be firm about it, provide a backup plan for the children. While they prefer you to say, "I'll be home tonight at eleven," they'll also accept, "I expect to be home by eleven, but if I'm not, I'll call your baby-sitter to tell her where I am."

Young children will be visibly relieved by your having a schedule and sticking to it. Older children, especially teenagers, may pretend that they're above such matters and couldn't care less where you go, how long you stay away, or when you get home. But just try being late once, and you'll get all sorts of remarks from them about your lateness. Moral: with all children, of whatever age, let them know exactly when you're going to be absent and when you will return. With preteens and adolescents, this will also illustrate for them why *you* get alarmed when *they* don't get home at the time they said they would.

Simplify!

As far as actual housekeeping goes—the million and one chores that everybody has to do and nobody likes—the one way to make life easier is simply to cut out as many of them as possible. No man (no woman, either, regardless of what the magazines say) has time for job, kids, and housework, too. Of the three, most of us would rather get rid of housework. And a lot of it is get-riddable. Nobody's holding a gun to your head to be Mr. Housekeeping of the Year. Who *says* you can't have hamburgers at every meal? *Why* do your undershirts have to be folded after you wash them? Is it really necessary to vacuum the living room every week?

Of course it's nice to have veal marsala whenever you want it and to have a drawerful of nicely folded underwear and spotless living room carpets . . . but how much do they really matter?

The point is, you've got to set your priorities. And if your job and your children come first (not to mention your self), then running the house simply has to take a backseat.

If you can avoid any time-consuming chores, then do so. Time is always better spent doing something you like than something you detest. Of course, if you're poor as a church mouse, then you have no choice but to get down on your knees and scrub the kitchen floor yourself. If you have any sort of financial leeway at all, how-ever, it's almost always good value to pay to have somebody scrub the floor for you.

That is, if you think the floor needs to be scrubbed at all.

This is where the idea of simplification comes in. If you can simplify your life by not scrubbing the kitchen floor at all or by scrubbing it only once in a blue moon, then why not? Just because your wife (or you yourself) used to keep the kitchen spotless and could be found with mop and pail every Wednesday morning doesn't mean you have to continue the tradition. A spot or two, or a spill mark and a grease stain, can usually wait a week or two before being attended to, especially when it's a case of taking time away from yourself or your children in order to mop up the glop. It's a case of not trying to be a paragon but just being the you that you are.

The Big Four of household maintenance are: shopping, cooking, cleaning, and doing laundry. There are a million more, of course (like walking the dog, fixing broken toys, sewing the button back on the shirt sleeve), but these are the big ones. Each can be radically simplified.

Shopping

- Go to the supermarket once a month and no more.
- Keep the freezer full of food for emergencies.
- Patronize a supermarket that will take orders over the phone and deliver directly to your house.
- Hire a teenager to do your shopping for you.
- Let your children do the shopping, if they're old enough and are interested.

Cooking

- Eat out a lot.
- Order Chinese food over the phone (with no MSG).
- Buy TV dinners (if you're on a budget) or take-out frozen delicacies from specialty stores (if you're not).
- Have your mother make several big casseroles for you every week.

Cleaning

- Hire a cleaning woman/man/teenager.
- Hire a cleaning service.
- Parcel out some or all of the household cleaning chores to the children in return for larger allowances.
- Keep your windows shut so that dust won't come in.

Laundry

- Get rid of all your clothes that need ironing; buy drip-dry.
- Get rid of clothes that need dry-cleaning (you can even get suits that don't need dry-cleaning).

- Hire a teenager to do your laundry for you.
- Don't do lots of little loads of laundry; do one big load, and if necessary buy more clothes so you can wait longer between.

Of course, if you enjoy doing laundry . . . well, then do it. Most of us enjoy doing at least one household chore. (In my own case, for instance, it's cooking. I don't mind spending four hours in the kitchen preparing a meal, but I get ornery after spending even five minutes with the iron.) If you like a chore, then it's no longer a chore. Also—and this is an added advantage—the children will probably pick up on your enthusiasm and perhaps want to get involved themselves. (That was certainly the case with my son. He loved to get his hands on the eggbeater, the mixer, the blender, or whatever I was using when I was in the kitchen.)

How Not to Be a Slave to Your Children

There's a standard scenario for weekend visits that's all too familiar to single fathers: the children arrive on Friday night and are greeted royally by Dad, then proceed to spend the weekend doing whatever they please while Dad does all the work.

"But they're only here for two days," Dad says in explanation of his masochistic behavior. "I feel guilty making them work."

What he really means, even though he doesn't come right out and say it, is that he's afraid deep down in his gut that if he makes them share any of the household work, they won't want to come back to see him anymore. This is the nameless fear that fathers simply refuse to face, since it's too unnerving. Instead, they go on playing the workhorse while the children stay plopped in front of the TV set.

This happens with practically all single fathers, not just weekend fathers. Whether he sees his children two days at a time or six months at a time, he always feels it's his job to do the work and the children's job to have the fun.

What he doesn't quite realize in all this is that he's defeating the primary purpose of children's visits: to be together as a family. If he's in the kitchen all the time, or running to the store to shop, or sitting behind the wheel of the car while he chauffeurs the children someplace or other, or doing the laundry, or setting the table, or any other tasks, then he's not really being with the kids.

The strange thing is how fathers allow themselves to change so radically when they get separated. While they were married, the household ran along accepted lines, with certain spoken or unspoken rules regulating everyone's behavior. All the family members, including the children, had certain responsibilities and knew what these responsibilities were. *After* the separation, however, Dad develops vast areas of insecurity. Suddenly the whole former way of life flies out the window. Children's responsibilities evaporate. They're pampered and indulged as though they were temperamental invalids.

Even if they used to expect to be asked to set the table, to take out the garbage, to help with the shopping, now they're treated to a field day. Dad abdicates his former position as head of the household and declines to the position of a sort of social director or glorified servant. When he sees the children, his position is strained and unnatural, and neither he nor the children know quite where they stand.

Needless to say, the situation isn't healthy for either the father or the children.

It all comes back to the basic position of being a single father: you and your children are a family, and when they are with you, they are at home. Your behavior, then, has to tell the children that this *is* a home, not a recreation center. Being a slave to your children sends them all the wrong signals.

The children should have responsibilities in your new home, just as they did in the old. They should be part of the household machinery, just as they used to be. Dad should simply let it be understood that the essentials of home life haven't changed; when the children are with him, they're still expected to take out the garbage or help with the dishes.

The children may (and probably will) whine shamelessly at these "unfair" duties and employ all sorts of subtle emotional blackmail to get you to do the work. Children soon learn that if they fuss or fume over being asked to do any work, you'll probably do the work yourself for fear of having an ugly blow-up on your hands or of losing their affection and goodwill. "Aw, Dad, do I have to? Mom doesn't make me." "Work, work, work! That's all I do around here. I'd rather be at Mom's." "I don't want to come here again next weekend if I can't watch TV."

When a household splits up, the sum total of work that has to be done in the two new households increases. There are now two homes to keep clean, two households' laundry to wash, two sets of meals to be cooked every day. But the total number of people inhabiting those two households hasn't changed: it's still Mom, Dad, and the children. The inescapable result is that everyone has to do more work. At least that's the way it should be. If the children don't pitch in, then Dad has to do it all, and he's sorely overburdened.

The children should share the work. This is the bottom line of the changed family structure. Dad will not only have to see that they maintain the same responsibilities they had before the split-up, but he'll also have to parcel out some of the added work that has been generated by having two households instead of one.

Children will be sore at this. "More work? When will I ever have any time to have fun?" Dad will have to use all his persuasiveness, not to mention his courage, to cope with the situation.

It won't be so bad if he is convinced of the rightness of his position—if he knows that it's a good thing for the children to have responsibilities—if he knows that responsibilities give a sense of belonging. If the children know that every week they're going to be expected to cook breakfast or pick up the laundry, they may not *like* it, but they know, indisputably, that they're part of a working household.

Aside from this, there are a few ways to slide into the new situation with a minimum of fuss and tribulation.

1. Gear children's responsibilities and chores to their ages and capabilities. If possible, don't assign them the "dumb" jobs that make them feel they're simply being exploited as cheap labor. Don't make them empty the wastebaskets if they could instead be doing the food shopping. Shopping is more responsible, more adult—more fun—and children will appreciate being considered worthy of it. When you're assigning a task, say, "I think you're old enough and smart enough to do this."

2. Be honest. "There's a certain amount of basic work that has to get done in this house, and I can't do it all. It's only fair that everyone share it." Don't imply that you're assigning tasks simply because you don't want to do them yourself. Don't assign them in a dictatorial way, as though you're assigning punishments. And don't imply that they have to do the work because Mom isn't around anymore to do it (it's demeaning to Mom to imply this, and it also makes the children think you're thrusting them into Mom's shoes, which can lead to neurotic confusion on their part).

3. Show your appreciation. This needn't be effusive praise ("Daddy's little girl is such a wonderful homemaker!"). On the contrary, it should be a simple person-to-person acknowledgment of assistance rendered.

4. If you can arrange tasks so that the family does them together, so much the better. Cooking meals lends itself to this: one person cooks, another sets the table, another prepares the food, another makes the dessert. Cleaning and doing laundry can also be done this way.

The more positive the work is, the better. Most tasks, even menial ones like shaking out the clothes and folding them, can be made into games. As usual, much depends on where your head is.

5. Let children swap tasks among themselves. This is especially handy with boring, menial chores. "There are a bunch of jobs that none of us wants to do," you say. "Therefore we're each going to take two of them, and we can then trade the tasks among us if we want to." Children don't mind doing chores so much if they see clearly that (a) they have a choice, and (b) the boring jobs are fairly and evenly distributed.

House Rules

In most married households, house rules are not explicit. Most of them are simply understood through long usage, because "we've always done it that way." The children have been taught that they must knock on closed doors before entering, that dirty boots are to be left on the porch, and that Mom and Dad shouldn't be disturbed before nine o'clock on Sunday morning. Of course, some rules occasionally get a very explicit airing: "How many times have I told you blasted kids to wash your hands before coming to the table?"

In single-parent households, everything is so different and new (at least at the start) that children may wonder if the old house rules have evaporated. They'll test you at every opportunity. They'll track mud on the carpet, they'll turn on the TV at seven-thirty in the morning, they'll eat their meals with dirty hands. And if you, through negligence or insecurity, don't pick them up on it, they'll assume that the rules don't apply anymore. Give 'em an inch and they'll take a mile.

Family rules and standards of behavior will have to be reaffirmed explicitly after the separation (and for months or years afterward, since the children tend to "forget"). If you don't let them know what is expected of them in terms of behavior, they may interpret this as meaning that you're out of control and incompetent at dealing with your new situation. Having house rules tells them that you're in control, and they need to know this. It gives them a sense of security when they need it most. If you let the house rules slide, they'll have the uneasy sense that their ship is being piloted by a captain who doesn't know where he's heading and is just drifting with the current.

Probably the best way to make house rules in a single-parent household is to negotiate them, at least to a degree, with the children. The children will be flattered to be consulted; it implies that you consider them mature and responsible human beings. "Okay, if you want an extra hour of TV on Saturday morning, you'll have to make a concession somewhere else—how about feeding the dog?" "If you want to play your music loud, that's okay, but you'll have to do it between three and five o'clock."

What Bothers Children
About Single-Parent Households

It's very interesting to actually ask children what, if anything, bothers them about living with Dad. I've asked lots of kids this question, and strangely enough, it's usually not the big emotional issues. They don't always say things like, "Dad doesn't pay enough attention to me anymore," or "I don't see as much of him as I'd like," or "I wish he and Mom would get back together again," or "I'm worried all the time."

The things children actually beef about are far more specific and concrete—four things in particular:

1. Dad's house. "It's so boring." "It's too small." "It's empty." "There's nothing to do there."

2. Packing. "It's such a nuisance to pack and unpack a suitcase every weekend to go to Dad's." "I always forget something."

3. Household rules. "Dad's always nagging me about something." "After I've been at Mom's, I forget how I'm supposed to act at Dad's."

4. Food. "We always have hot dogs, never anything else." "The food is always burned." "The food's always cold." "There's nothing to eat for snacks."

Actually, most single fathers are terribly relieved to hear that children have such relatively innocuous complaints. It's easy to remedy most of them, whereas it would not be easy to fix a situation in which a child was saying, "I'm so sad because I don't see my Daddy very often."

Dad's House

When children complain about where Dad lives, it's usually to say that the place is boring. It's not as big, not as well furnished, not as "lived in" as the family house they're used to. The complaints stop as soon as Dad takes steps to make the place "interesting":

Furnish it as fully as possible. It shouldn't look sterile and impersonal, like a motel room. If money is a problem, either rent furniture or buy cheap "fun" furniture like plastic inflatable armchairs.

Bring some furniture from your old family home if possible. (Your wife isn't entitled to it all.) It not only helps fill the empty rooms, it also gives a homey, familiar air to the place.

Beg furniture from your parents. Raid their attic if they have one. Or "borrow" the furniture from their unused bedroom.

Involve the children in the furnishing and decorating of your new place. Ask them where the couch would look best. Ask them to paint the living room walls. Ask them to tack paintings on the wall.

This not only saves you labor, but it gives the children a stake in the new place and makes it seem less unfamiliar and empty to them.

When children complain that there's nothing to do at Dad's, they usually mean that (1) they just haven't gotten used to the place yet, and (2) they don't know the neighborhood yet and feel like strangers. At the start, provide as much in-house entertainment as possible. Make sure they bring their watercolors, their guitar, their kite (or any other favorite amusement) when they stay with you. And suggest that they help you explore the neighborhood. Older children will do this anyway, but younger ones may need a helping push to get them out of the house and onto the sidewalk. Once they start exploring the neighborhood, they'll find amusements of their own (which usually amounts to finding out how the other children in the neighborhood are staying amused) and they'll stop complaining so much about having nothing to do at your place.

As a last alternative, if your place is an absolute bummer and there's nothing you can do about it, then try a switch with your wife. Instead of bringing the kids to your place, you go to them at your wife's place. Your ex can go stay at your dreary abode for the duration, or at her parents', or with understanding friends. This may be a nuisance, but it may salvage the situation until you can move into a more suitable place.

Packing

Children are annoyed by the logistics of going back and forth between two homes. You can hardly blame them; anybody would be bored with packing a suitcase once a week (or once a month, or whatever) and trekking back and forth like a commuter. So anything that can be done to streamline the operation will go a long way toward making the children happier with the situation.

—Don't nag. When you pick up the kids to come to your place, they are often not ready. (And when it's time for you to take them back to Mom's, they're often not ready then, either.) It rarely does any good to complain. It only makes the children resent the move even more. Instead, concentrate your energies on making the move more efficient.

—When you pick them up, have a checklist of items that you especially want them to bring along—or items that they often forget. Read the checklist aloud to make sure they've packed everything.

—Make a routine of repacking when it's time to return to Mom's, so that you don't forget anything. Provide color-coded checklists, or let the children work in relays. Play the drill sergeant. "Shirt." "Check." "Guitar." "Check." "Math book." "Check." This will work for young children (who have the most trouble with packing), but it will be too babyish for older children and teenagers.

—Decide in conference with the children which items it would be worth keeping at both homes. If the children are going to be with you for more than two days at a time, for instance, they should keep duplicate sets of these items in both homes:

toothbrush

hairbrush

toiletries (if they have any particular favorites)

pajamas

medicine (if they have a chronic condition)

pencils

rulers

dictionary

socks (always an absolute necessity)

—Negotiate a rule regarding items they accidentally leave behind when you pick them up. Things often get left behind, but you can't always be driving back to Mom's to pick them up. Thrash out a rule with the children. They should know where they stand.

"If it gets left behind, you'll just have to do without it."

"If you forget it, I'm not going back for it except in life-or-death cases."

"I'll turn the car around and go back to your mother's if we're less than halfway to my place."

Usually the basic problem is that the children have a hard time remembering the different rules in each of their two households. Thus, when they first arrive at your place, their heads may still be operating as if they were at Mom's, and they'll accidentally infringe some of your rules. Having to switch behavior is a nuisance in itself, but it's even more of a problem if you blow up at them or act annoyed at the inadvertent transgressions. When you feel like scolding, remember that the shoe is sometimes on the other foot and you may be the one having difficulty adjusting to the company.

—Give them time. It'll take them a day or two to get back into the groove of the routine at your place. Of course, if they're only with you for two days, then they may never adjust, and you'll just have to face reality and moderate your demands to the point where they *can* make the adjustment.

—Try to involve them in the making of the household rules in the first place. Don't issue them like God giving Moses the ten commandments. If the kids have had a hand in making the rules —even a very minor hand—they won't be so apt to forget them.

If you handle the situation with reasonable aplomb, the children will gain the useful skill of being adept socially, at gracefully adjusting their behavior to the particular environment they're in. As for you, it will increase your art of expression, since it takes more skill to negotiate gracefully than simply to mandate rules with no explanation.

Food

Food, like decor, is a concrete, tangible subject that looms large in children's minds. In the most basic sense, they won't feel at home at your place if they don't feel nourished there. And with them, nourishment is not a dry, theoretical subject; it's a straightforward matter of what's on their plates for dinner. If you're a lousy cook, or an unimaginative one, or just not as good as Mom, they'll feel shortchanged when they're with you.

And you can't really solve the problem by always taking them out to dinner. That's not healthy for your home life or your wallet. More palatable alternatives (in both senses of the word):

—Buy prepared food. If nothing else, you'll have variety, and the food won't always be burned.

—Have a friend, a neighbor, your mother, or anyone bake casseroles for you. This is a notch above prepared foods like TV dinners or chicken pies.

—Practice a couple of unusual specialties to make when the kids are with you, something they don't usually get at Mom's or anywhere else. Even if you're not much of a cook, you can usually manage to master a couple of dishes so that you can turn them out with reasonable success. Anything out of the ordinary will do. Shish kebab, for instance, or waffles, or pecan pie (you can use a store-bought crust), or chicken roasted on a revolving barbecue. The children will look forward to their visits with you if they know they're going to get one of these interesting specialties.

Birthdays and Holidays

Birthdays are always a problem in single-parent households, and so are holidays. Where will Johnnie spend his birthday, with Mom or with Dad? Will Mom or Dad have Melissa for Christmas? Which household should have the children for the summer vacation? And so forth.

Because these are such important times, Mom and Dad often find themselves at loggerheads over who'll have the children. The best way to avoid conflicts is to plan far in advance. Then there's plenty of time to negotiate and there's less chance of last-minute disappointments or accusations. ("But I thought the kids were coming *here* for Thanksgiving!" "But Davie spent his birthday with you last year; now it's my turn." "It's too late to change plans. Sorry.") If you want to go on a long trip with the children in August, it makes sense to broach the subject to their mother in January. Bat it back and forth until you come to an agreement. Don't leave it until July, when everything has to be resolved in a rush and feelings may get bruised.

Possibilities for Birthdays

—Alternate the children's birthdays from year to year; Mom has Jennifer this year, Dad next.

—Celebrate the birthday twice—on the actual day at Mom's, and the next weekend at Dad's. Or let one parent celebrate the birthday, the other the christening.

—Split the day of the birthday. The child can have the afternoon at Mom's, the evening at Dad's; or an afternoon party with Dad and an evening slumber party at Mom's.

Possibilities for Holidays

—Alternate Christmas, Hanukkah, New Year's, or any other important holiday from year to year: this year at Dad's, next year at Mom's.

—Trade off year-end holidays: Christmas with Mom, Thanksgiving with Dad; Hanukkah with Mom, New Year's with Dad.

—Add a second holiday: celebrate Christmas at one home and Twelfth Night at the other.

—Split the holiday itself: the afternoon at Mom's, the evening at Dad's.

5.

DEALING WITH YOUR EX-WIFE (YOUR CHILDREN'S MOTHER)

Ideally a book about single fathers wouldn't need a chapter about ex-wives. After all, the whole point of divorce and single fathering is to get *rid* of your wife. She should no longer be in the picture. It should be just you and the children.

If only it were so easy.

Unfortunately, the ex-wife is always very much in the picture. You have to deal with her whether you want to or not, and her existence, frankly, may be nothing but a pain in the ass to you. (If this sounds unfair or sexist, let me say quickly that the opposite is just as true: your existence may be a pain in the ass to her.) When you separate, your relationship with her is far from over. She still pops up in your life in all sorts of ways: you have to send her money every month; you get nostalgic about her and wish you were still married; you hate her and want to "get even"; you have to make awkward conversation with her when you pick up the children at her place; the memory of her lingers in your mind and makes you get soppy with longing.

I can remember times in my own separation when I wished my wife had actually died. It would have been more final, it would have settled things. (Actually, I was just looking for an easy way out.)

In a perfect world, we'd be able to wave a magic wand and our ex-spouses would disappear from our lives. Alas, it's not a perfect world, and so we have to deal with them as best we can. That phrase, *as best we can,* isn't always easy to live up to. In fact, it's often damn difficult. This chapter frankly is a counsel of perfection. The advice I'm going to give is good (it ought to be—it's been tested by enough of us), but only a superman could follow it to the letter, day in and day out.

It's a case of do as I say, not as I do. Certainly I myself haven't been able to follow my own advice with any kind of consistency, though heaven knows I've tried. I always had good intentions. I knew how I should act with my ex-wife, but when it came right down to it, I often fell into the bad old habits I warn about in this chapter. After a while, I got philosophical about it. It's like dieting: you can't be 100 percent perfect. You'll slip occasionally and go on a chocolate binge, but if you're reasonably careful most of the time, things will eventually work out in your favor. Time and maturity on both sides do eventually tend to win.

If your relationship with your ex-wife is perfectly unclouded, then you can glide right over this chapter. Even if, as in most of our cases, it's a mix of the good and the bad, you won't find much here on the good side of things. We're concentrating on the bad side because that's the area that has to be fixed.

Let Her Go:
or, How Not to Be Obsessed with Your Ex

At times, especially right after the separation, you'll be light-years away from forgetting your ex-wife. Just the opposite, you'll be obsessed with her. You can't live *with* her, but you may not yet know how to live *without* her. She sticks in your mind . . . she gets under your skin . . . she's a burr under your saddle. Inevitably you find yourself rehashing your marriage to try to answer that fruitless question, "What went wrong?" You'll have wildly conflicting emotions about her. You'll hate her, then you'll want her back; you'll never want to see her again, then you'll fall into a daydream about the good old days of your marriage; you'll cry when you think of her, then you'll vow you want to get even with her.

But . . . you did separate from her. One or both of you decided the two of you could not live together. That's the essential point to keep in mind when you can't seem to get your wife out of your mind. You've got to start changing the equation of your life so that only you and the children remain. You've got to bring the emotional reality into line with the legal reality. Which brings us to the First Law of Dealing with Ex-Wives:

Rule # 1: Let her go!

Let her disappear into her own separate existence. Let her have her own life. Let her smoothly drift out of your mind.

Easier said than done. It's hard to stop thinking about her, especially if she arouses violent emotions in you. If the divorce was a bitter one, your anger with her will probably last a long time. Even if the divorce was relatively amicable, you'll feel occasional twinges of jealousy, hurt, anger, nostalgia, and all the rest of those emotions that tag along after separated fathers like mangy dogs.

There are four particularly annoying ways you may find yourself still tied emotionally to your wife after the divorce:

You're jealous of her.

You compete with her.

You hate her.

You depend on her for emotional support.

Competitiveness, hate, jealousy, emotional dependency—they are all forms of continuing intimacy. If you still compete with your ex-wife, or hate her, or are jealous of her, or desire her for emotional support, then you're not yet free of her. You're not your own person. True divorce hasn't taken place. It says you're divorced on a piece of paper, but you're not divorced in your head yet.

To a certain extent, time alone will cure you of these emotional obsessions with your ex-wife. But the process will go a lot faster if you monitor yourself constantly and try to speed the cure as you go along.

Danger Signs of Lingering Intimacy

• referring to her as "my wife"
• being involved in *any* legal action against her

- talking about her a lot in conversation (even if it's to say how much you dislike her)
- rehashing your marriage in your mind instead of thinking about your new life
- still having a key to her home (or she having one to yours)
- still storing some of your personal items at her place
- having daydreams of violence or revenge against her
- dreaming about her
- asking (or pumping) mutual friends for information about what she's doing
- making a point of keeping sentimental mementoes like love letters
- finding excuses to telephone her
- picking fights with her
- avoiding any issues with her because you're afraid of her reaction
- blaming her for being the basic cause of your problems
- pumping the children about life at her place

Competitiveness

Competitiveness arises when you have a need to "prove" that the divorce wasn't your fault, that she was the one really to blame for the failure of the marriage. So you try to show—to her, to the children, to your friends, and most of all to yourself—that you're a better person and a better parent than she is. You try to be both a better father *and* a better mother than your ex-wife. You're always comparing yourself to her, using her as a sort of measuring rod for yourself as you play your game of one-upmanship.

Competitiveness is not as violent an emotion as hate or jealousy or as insidious a one as emotional dependency, and of the four, it's probably the easiest to overcome.

First, of course, you have to become conscious of what you're doing, that is, that you *are* being competitive. Admit that you're trying to prove a point: you're trying to impress everyone, including yourself, with how blameless and wonderful you are. It's a backhanded way of proclaiming, "The divorce wasn't my fault!"

If you can admit this, then you won't have a hard time admitting to yourself that logically, competitiveness is pointless and silly. It gets you nowhere. Trying to prove you're a better parent than your ex—or a better provider—or more responsible—or more reliable—or just more fun to be with—or more adult—won't make any difference to your children or to the world in general (and it certainly won't convince your ex-wife). Your kids won't love you more for it; they love you anyway. And it won't make them love your ex-wife less; they love you *both*.

The simple solution is to *be yourself.* Why not just accept this and save yourself the trouble of trying to set yourself an impossibly high standard in the hope of beating your ex-wife at an imaginary game. After all, your divorce did not occur because one of you was "better" or "worse" than the other. There were lots of reasons, often very complicated ones that you may not completely understand. Trying to play rating games now with your ex-wife absurdly oversimplifies a complex situation.

Every time you catch yourself comparing yourself in any way with your ex, just laugh at yourself and say, "What does it matter?" Relax and start acting like your old self.

Hate

Hate rears its ugly head when a divorce brings out all the latent animosity existing between a husband and wife. Hate is actually a form of lingering intimacy—negative intimacy. Some couples after divorce become more closely bound by hate than they ever were by love during their marriage. Hatred of your ex-wife can take the form of brooding over daydreams of vengeance, bad-mouthing her to the children, being rude to her when you meet in person, blaming her for the divorce, accusing her of "taking you to the cleaners," and dumping on her in any other ways you can think of.

There are no easy answers to curing this problem, unfortunately. Too often, a man doesn't *want* to be cured—he gets too much gratification out of hating his wife. Being angry at her can be awfully satisfying, frankly. It makes a man feel superior, powerful, relieved, and righteous all at once.

Before you can make any progress against hate, you have to realize that hating your wife does more harm than good. It's like scratching a case of poison ivy—it feels so good, but it only spreads the poison. Hating your wife is the same—it gives powerful emotional gratification, but it eventually saddles you with festering psychological problems that hurt more than they help.

The basic problem with hate and anger is that they keep you from living your own life. You're focusing all your emotional energy on your ex-wife when you should be focusing it on yourself. Until you realize this deep down in your gut, it's hard to give up hating her.

Often hate and anger are cover-ups for sadness, hurt, emptiness, loneliness. It's easier to get angry than to admit to a bad case of the blues. But if you can get under the hate and anger to the emotions underneath and work on *them*, then the force of your hate will tend to abate.

Jealousy

Jealousy is a problem when you can't stand the idea of your ex-wife being with other men, even though you're not her husband anymore. You may constantly wonder what she's up to, whom she's with, what she's doing. And the idea of another man in the bed *you* used to occupy makes you sick with rage.

The more you know about your ex, the more jealous you'll be. If someone says to you, "I saw Christine the other day," you'll wonder if Christine was with another man. If a male friend tells you he had a conversation with her, you'll immediately fantasize that they're sleeping together. And if your ex has a boyfriend, you'll go bonkers whenever his name comes up in conversation.

In these cases, it pays to be ignorant. You can't get jealous about what you don't know. (Well, actually you can, but we have to draw the line somewhere.) The less you know about your ex-wife—her home life, her habits, her new friends—the happier you'll be.

So don't ask mutual friends, "What's Christine up to these days?" Don't ask the children, "How's your mother?" Don't ask her, "How's your life going?" Don't ask any questions at all that even obliquely could lead to the subject of her personal life. If the children innocently chatter on about her, change the subject or go into the other room. If your friends insist on bringing up her name in conversation, ask them, bluntly if necessary, to stop. (If they still do it, drop them—at least temporarily.)

Even if you secretly fear that people are laughing at you behind their backs, *ignore them.* Just keep smiling and remember, ignorance is bliss.

Usually this works. If it doesn't—if you find yourself having violent fantasies about her love life all the time, with no encouragement—you have a bad case. This frankly is probably too much for you to cure yourself. The solution: therapy. The relief will be amazing.

Emotional Dependency

Emotional dependency may be a problem if you used to depend on your wife for comfort and companionship, and now that you're divorced, you still find yourself longing for her whenever you get down in the dumps and need a bit of tender loving care. (Sometimes you'll wonder how you could possibly have divorced her.)

One of the best options I've ever found for dealing with this problem comes from an unlikely source: Alcoholics Anonymous. When you come right down to it, emotional dependency is a little like alcoholism, except that you turn to your wife (or the memory of her) for relief instead of to the bottle. Like an alcoholic, you're likely to do this when you're feeling emotionally low and need an emotional pick-me-up or shot in the arm. AA finds that these situations crop up most commonly when you are:

H—hungry
A—angry
L—lonely
T—tired

AA calls this the HALT syndrome. Like an alcoholic, you'll probably find that your bouts of emotional dependency on your wife come when you, too, are hungry, angry, lonely, or tired. That's when you'll find yourself wishing she were with you—nagging mutual friends for news of her—questioning the children for information about her—in general, trying to get emotionally closer to her. The "cure," according to AA, is simply to recognize these four circumstances in which you're likely to be vulnerable and then, when you feel yourself slipping into one of them, tell yourelf, "HALT!"

It's really more of a warning device than a cure. But it does work. It alerts you to the fact that you're in the danger zone and that unless you do something to pep up your mood, you may sink into a full-fledged emotional funk. Like an alcoholic, you have to stop yourself from taking even one sip of your particular poison.

What you need is diversion of some sort. An alcoholic, instead of taking a drink, may smoke a cigarette or chew a piece of gum. The "emotional junkie"—the person emotionally dependent on his ex-wife—needs the stimulus of other people. When you find yourself in the HALT situation, try to do something with another person: call a friend on the phone—have a party—go out to dinner with an interesting woman—even hunt up a one-night stand. Or go to a movie or read a novel—it's better than nothing.

Sometimes even a sharp cutoff will do the trick. When I used to catch myself daydreaming about my ex-wife and longing for the old days of my marriage, I pulled myself up short and said to myself, "Thanks, Linda, for the memories. But now it's good-bye." Even that simple little phrase often was enough to yank me back from the quicksands of emotional dependency.

Chalk up a point for yourself every time you catch yourself before falling into an emotionally dependent mood and successfully divert yourself. Each time you do this, it becomes easier.

Dealing with Your Ex

Since there's no way you can avoid dealing with your ex-wife—not just now but for many years to come—you've got to work out a reasonably practical way of interacting with her on an everyday level. "Impossible!" you may say. I can hear the chorus of reasons:

"I hate her."

"She refuses to talk to me."

"I never want to see her again."

"It's impossible to have a sane conversation with her."

"She drives me crazy."

"She always lies."

"I'm too angry to talk to her."

"We always end up yelling at each other."

"She's too irrational to deal with."

"We can never agree on anything."

"She can't think straight."

"I can't talk to her."

Well, yes. All this may be true, but you *still* have to deal with her. There's simply no way to avoid it. You can't just say, "Let the lawyers handle it." Unless, of course, you're filthy rich, in which case you don't need this book to advise you: you've already got a battery of legal eagles to advise you at several hundred dollars an hour.

On the most basic level, you can't avoid a certain amount of contact with your ex-wife, at least until the children are grown. Almost all single fathers have to deal with their ex's in more than one of the following ways:

—picking up the children at her place for the weekend

—planning which of you will have the children for holidays

—attending school functions, such as graduations, which involve both parents

—explaining why this month's child support check is late (or sending a new check to replace the one she lost)

—making joint decisions about sending the kids to college

—revising your separation agreement

—renegotiating alimony or child support if her financial situation changes

—disciplining the children

—answering her requests for more money

—handling serious problems involving the children, such as illness, psychological problems, failure in school, etc.

—saying hello to her on the phone when you call the children at her place (or she calls them at yours)

If these meetings and interactions are to be relatively equable and workable, you've got to work out a way of dealing with her that avoids anger, strong emotions, recriminations, or any of the other traps that turn innocuous social encounters into prizefight spectacles. Which brings us to the Second Law of Dealing with Ex-Wives:

Rule # 2: Put your relationship on a strictly business basis.

This is almost always the safest way for two ex-spouses to deal with each other—to be cool, formal, and businesslike and banish emotions from their dealings. The most basic task after separation is to "unlearn" your intimacy with your wife and retreat to a safer, more impersonal relationship with her. The secret is to get past the "enemy" stage. It can and does happen: no longer lovers, not enemies, but mutual business acquaintances.

Optimistic single fathers sometimes say they want to work on a new relationship with their wives and become "just good friends." If they've got to have contact with each other, they reason, doesn't it make sense to stay friendly and have something more than a cold business relationship? Yes, it can work, but it takes time. Usually a lot of water has to pass under the bridge before you and your ex-wife can completely reshape your roles to the point of being nothing more and nothing less than friends.

In the early stages, it's much safer all around to retreat to the secure ground of a strictly business relationship.

In that case, how do you go about it?

Understanding Where She's Coming From

If you really want to set up a workable relationship, it helps to know something about her motivations as well as your own. If you have some idea of why she does all the things you object to—lying, flaring up, shedding tears, refusing to talk—you can be a little more tolerant in dealing with her. (Of course, it works both ways: she has to learn to be tolerant of your failings.) Both of you were and are vulnerable, and the trust level between you is probably at an all-time low.

It goes without saying that she's hurt, resentful, and wounded—just as you are. But underneath all this, there may be something else that you have never realized: she may be afraid of you. Which may be the cause of some of her actions that seem inexplicable or unjustified to you.

Oh, she's not necessarily physically afraid. It's not usually an obvious kind of fear that she has. But if you, the male, have been the "dominant" partner during your marriage, then she may have learned a kind of deep-down wariness of your temper, your power in the relationship, your control of the financial pursestrings, or your jealousy.

And now, though the marriage is ended, it may be hard for her to get over these old gut reactions. Also, in most cases, she's financially dependent on you, and she may have the fear (real or imagined) that you may someday cut off her financial support or try to make her pay tenfold for it emotionally.

Of course, fear can work both ways, and there may be times when you fear her for some reason. But the balance usually tips the scales of fear toward the wife's side of the fence. It's hard for a worried or fearful ex-wife to be completely calm, composed, and rational in your presence. She may be unintentionally rude or sharp. She may lie. She may be evasive.

If you're sensitive to this, it will make it easier for you to overlook the way she acts. If, for instance, you've ever gone for a job interview and been so nervous that you came across as harsh and abrasive—or lied to a job interviewer and told him what you thought he wanted to hear—or tried to second-guess him so that you gave the "right" answers—then you have some idea of what an ex-wife may feel when she has to deal with her former spouse.

Blueprint for a Practical Relationship

Probably the easiest way to get a handle on your new relationship with your ex is to think of yourselves as business partners—partners in the business of bringing up and supporting the children. The children are your only connection. You're going halves on them, so to speak, agreeing to collaborate with each other in the enterprise of bringing the children to maturity.

You may not want to be partners with your ex, but you are. Even if she is "hopeless," "totally illogical," "off the wall," "sick," and so on, you're going to have to work with her. The fact that you don't get along with each other shouldn't stand in the way of your doing business together. It doesn't matter if you hate or distrust her. People regularly do business with people they dislike or distrust. Emotional incompatibility doesn't stop people from doing business together—when the deal is important enough.

Your children are certainly an important enough "deal" for you to expend a lot of time and energy in forging a practical working relationship with your ex-wife.

Building a businesslike relationship with an ex-wife is basically the same as building a business relationship with anyone else. It may take longer, and it may be more awkward and more painful, but it does work. The basic characteristics of the relationship will be the same as for any other relationship in the business world:

Formality. You make appointments in advance and meet on neutral ground. When you have meetings, you have specific subjects to talk about. You don't get together to chat.

Politeness. You don't make rude comments, interrupt each other, or fly off the handle. You don't make scenes.

Impersonality. You don't make personal comments, and you don't ask personal questions of the other party.

No unwarranted assumptions. You don't assume the other person will automatically know what you're talking about or expect her to read your mind. You're explicit and precise. You don't say, "You know what I mean, or you certainly ought to know—we lived together long enough."

Written agreements. You put it in writing whenever appropriate. You don't operate by the seat of the pants. You sign contracts or other agreements when called for (each situation is treated individually, of course). You send notes confirming the substance of important phone calls. You put it in writing so there won't be misunderstandings in the future.

Negotiation. You deal with the other person to find a middle ground you can both live with. You don't issue ultimatums. You don't treat meetings as confrontations. (You must decide beforehand what you want and to what extent you're willing to bend.)

Sticking to the point. When you call the other party or have a meeting, you don't wander to extraneous subjects. You have two or three specific subjects for discussion at that meeting, and you stick to them.

Naturally, you'll feel awkward in trying to be cool and businesslike with the person you've lived with on a deeply emotional basis for an important chunk of your life. You've confided in her, laughed with her, slept with her—and now you're trying to treat her as a stranger. Any new relationship takes getting used to, but this one takes more than most. You'll probably feel silly the first few times you call your ex to arrange a meeting or say "May I come in?" when you arrive at her door. We all go through it. But it's better to be a little too formal—even if you feel embarrassed—than to risk misunderstandings by taking things for granted.

There may be times, too, when both you and your ex happen to be in particularly good moods and you can enjoy a more friendly get-together that's just like old times. There's nothing wrong with this. But the minute any undercurrents of anger or hurt or regret (or even too many warm feelings) begin to come to the surface again, it's time to beat a retreat to the safety of the business relationship.

Alas, there's a big distance between saying, "I'm going to be businesslike" and actually putting it into practice. The problem is that it's not always easy to transfer our business behavior to the personal side of our lives. It's easy to read a rule that says "Be impersonal," not so easy to translate that into actual practice.

So, enough theory. Here are some specific tricks of the trade that translate theory into practice.

—Make an appointment with her when you have something important to discuss. Don't just call her on the phone and start to talk. In the first place, it's more businesslike to make an appointment. In the second, if you spring the subject on her unawares, you may catch her at a bad time, when she's not willing or able to listen to you, in which case your chances of having a satisfactory discussion are zilch. In the third place, *you* may not be rational when you grab the telephone and dial without waiting for a proper appointment.

—Don't expect thanks. This is business, remember? You and your ex aren't in business to offer each other emotional support and gratification. If you figure you'll be a nice guy and let her have the kids for Christmas, don't be surprised—or upset—if you get small thanks for it. It would be nice if she thanked you profusely for being so accommodating, but she's not under any obligation to. And if you only agreed to the arrangement because you were fishing for praise and a figurative pat on the back, then you weren't acting businesslike yourself. If you've gotten used to expecting a lot of emotional support from your wife, this readjustment won't be easy or pleasant.

—When you get together with your ex to discuss important matters, stick to the point. If necessary, write out an agenda for yourselves, so you'll know exactly what you have to talk about. Then stick to the point. If you and she have set up a meeting to hash out the matter of sending the kids to camp next summer, don't let yourself slide off into a conversation about whether or not she'll have enough money for a new TV set. If she strays from the subject at hand, don't sneer and say, "Can we *please* stick to the point!" Steer the conversation back into its proper channel politely with a neutral comment such as, "But to get back to the matter of summer camp . . ."

—When you go to pick up the children at her place, knock on the door and wait to be invited in. Don't barge in. You're a guest now, not a husband, and you have no special privileges on her "territory." Even if she gives you a silly look and says, "For goodness sake, you don't have to knock," knock anyway. If one of the children opens the door and says, "Daddy! Come and look at my new kitten!" it's better to find an excuse to wait at the door until your ex appears. True, it is the child's house, and he does have a right to invite you in, but there's no sense in risking Mom's disapproval if you can help it.

And if she doesn't invite you into the house, don't get offended. Even if you think she's being rude, just stand there on the porch and keep smiling. She probably has a perfectly good reason for not inviting you in (one that may have nothing to do with you).

Also, pleasantness is contagious, and as long as either one of you is smiling and polite, it'll tend to make the encounter go well.

—When you're at her place, don't lapse into old habits. Don't be overfamiliar. If you want to use the bathroom, ask. If you want to make a phone call, ask.

—Don't phone her at odd hours. If she's at home during the day ("business hours"), then call her from nine to five. If she works during the day, ask her when and where (home or office) she prefers to take calls, then abide by her wishes.

—If you're ever in doubt as to what her behavior means, give her the benefit of the doubt. You may think she's being intentionally snide or rude or petty or obstructive, but she may only be nervous or upset. That cynical look may just be intestinal gas pain. Don't get defensive.

Be especially careful about things you hear about her from the kids or other third parties. Most of the time you won't be getting an accurate report. If a friend tells you, "Gerri called you a boor," take it with a grain of salt. Give her the benefit of the doubt. She may have said nothing of the kind.

—Don't have long meetings with her. The longer the two of you are together, the greater the chances you'll slip into unpleasantness. This means you shouldn't try to settle a lot at one meeting. Don't try to discuss doctor bills *and* your child's trouble in school *and* your mother-in-law's operation *and* the problems with the separation agreement all at the same meeting. You'd be tempting fate. Discuss only one or two of the issues, and save the rest for another time. And as soon as you've finished discussing those two issues, leave.

—Don't communicate via third parties. If you have a message for her, don't ask a mutual friend to deliver it, no matter how convenient this may be. Third-party messages are too easy to misunderstand. You can never be sure the message will arrive just as you sent it. If the message you mean to send is, "Can I have the kids this weekend?", it could get delivered as, "He wants the kids this weekend," which may sound like a demand to your ex and offend her with a demanding tone that you never intended to convey.

And if she sends you messages through third parties, be careful in interpreting them. Call her to confirm what she meant. Don't shout, "Caroline tells me you won't let me see the kids this weekend!" Just say, "I wanted to check on your message about this weekend." Better yet, ask her to communicate with you directly whenever she has anything to say.

—Keep conversations unemotional. If you find that you always flare up when you meet your ex in person, then use the telephone instead. If this doesn't work, write letters to each other.

—If you have lots of misunderstandings with your ex, then put things in writing. This will prevent either of you singing that old refrain, "He/she is unreliable. He/she says he/she will do something, and then he/she doesn't." If your ex says on the phone that she's willing for you to have the kids on Thanksgiving, then send her a short note saying, "I just wanted to confirm that we'd agreed I could have the children. . . ." Then if there has been any kind of misunderstanding, she can call you and say, "No, that is not what we agreed." But at any rate, neither of you will be able later to accuse the other of negligence or willful misunderstanding.

—If your relations with her are really strained, keep records of all your phone calls, letters, and the like. They may come in handy if you ever have to go to court or arbitration. Keep a log of the date of your calls and the subjects you discussed, and keep copies of your letters to her.

—Don't assume the old ways of your marriage are still in force. Don't take anything for granted. Even if you "always did it that way," you can't assume you'll do it that way now. Use your creativity and treat this venture as a wholly new experience.

—Don't expect miracles. Especially, don't expect your ex to be a person she is not. If she's disorganized and unbusinesslike, divorce won't change her. You'll just have to work around this. After all, some businesspeople are unbusinesslike, too. (Just remember she's aware of your shortcomings, too, and you're not involved in a contest to see who's "best.")

—Accusations and name calling never accomplish anything.

"You're an idiot!" "You're trying to alienate the kids from me!" "You're spending *my* money on your lover!" Outbursts like these won't get you anywhere, and they'll just make your ex angry and uncooperative. There's a good antidote for this. Instead of making accusations, which focuses the attention on *her,* simply talk about your feelings, which focuses the attention on you. For instance, instead of shouting, "You're damned insensitive!" say, "It hurts me when you say that." Instead of "You're poisoning the kids' minds against me," say, "I can't help worrying that the kids are drifting away from me." This may sound vulnerable and unenterprising, but at least it doesn't cause a flare-up. You can still talk. Accusations only bring conversation to an end. (Even if she *is* insensitive, or if she *is* poisoning the kids' minds against you, you don't think your accusations will make her admit it, do you?)

—Respect her privacy. Of course you'll want to know what she's feeding the children—how she's spending her (your!) money— who her friends are—what she talks about with the children— whom she's sleeping with. But don't ask. It's none of your business now. Indirect questions are even worse: "Did you get that promotion at your job?" (meaning "If you got a raise, I'm going to reduce the alimony payments"), "How did the children like the trip with you and Bert?" (meaning "Are you thinking of marrying Bert?"), "I understand the children say you've bought a new bed" (meaning "Whom are you sleeping with?"). She'll realize what you're doing and she'll resent it. Constant violation of her privacy will only make her uptight and uncooperative. If you keep away religiously from the subject of her personal life, she'll feel more like relaxing with you and being more cooperative.

—If there are times when you and your ex simply cannot do business with each other—or if there are certain subjects that inevitably provoke a fiery confrontation between you—then you may need outside help. When you're as far apart from each other as labor and management during a strike, then try arbitration. Find someone to mediate your dispute—someone whose decision you'll both abide by—preferably a professional marriage counselor or arbitrator.

The bottom line of your new relationship with your ex-wife is mutual respect. Let's face it, back at the beginning, you wanted her to be your lifelong companion and the mother of your children. Whatever you saw in her then is still there.

During my own separation, I was always forced to admit that my ex-wife deserved my respect, if for nothing else than the fact that she—like me—loved our child. Sometimes the respect level of our relationship was higher than at others, and sometimes it dipped pretty low, but it was always *there*. It was a positive thing that provided the foundation for our eventual good working relationship.

How Not to Have a Discussion

Separated people seem to have an almost endless battery of remarks that are guaranteed to inflame, outrage, or infuriate ex-spouses. And it's so tempting to use them. But if you do, it's good-bye to any chance of having a logical, sane discussion. Tears or tantrums or icy silence are the inevitable results. So here's a list of some of the powder-keg responses that lead to blow-ups:

SWEEPING GENERALIZATIONS

"Do you always have to get mad when . . . !"

"Can't you ever . . . ?"

"You are the most illogical person I've ever met!"

THREATS

"If you dare do that, you won't see another penny of my money!"

"Just try that once, and I'll kidnap the children from you."

SNIDE PUT-DOWNS

"I see you're still serving spaghetti to the kids."

"You really can't seem to pull yourself together, can you?"

"What's the matter with you? Can't you discipline your own son?"

"You're a mother. You're supposed to know about things like that."

ACCUSATIONS

"You don't care about anyone but yourself!"

"You don't give a damn about the kids!"

"You're just plain selfish!"

CHANGING THE SUBJECT

"What do you mean, the kids are out of control? *You're* out of control!"

"I'll think about paying alimony when you think about letting me see the kids more often."

"I neglect the kids?! What about the time *you* . . . ?"

CUT-OFFS

"I don't want to talk about it!"

"This discussion is pointless."

"You're too illogical. I can't talk to you."

"If you say one more word, I'll walk out!"

LECTURING

"For God's sake, don't keep giving her chocolate. It'll make her break out."

"Honestly, haven't you learned yet that you should never do that?"

"Here, let me *show* you how to do it."

AMATEUR PSYCHOLOGIZING

"You're just saying that because you have guilty feelings and you're really hoping I'll. . . ."

"Can't you see you're projecting your own guilt feelings onto me?"

Children in the Crossfire

The trouble with flare-ups and disagreements between ex-husband and ex-wife is that they often spill over and affect the children. If you and your children's mother are gunning for each other, you'll score plenty of hits on each other, but you'll be shooting so wildly that you'll probably blast the kids, too.

If there were no other reason for trying to get on a better basis with your ex, this would be reason enough. The children didn't ask you to get divorced, and they don't deserve to suffer unnecessarily for it. There are dozens of ways you can unintentionally put your children in the direct line of fire between you and their mother:

Bad-mouthing her. "What's your mother been feeding you—dog food?" "Your mother never could balance a checkbook." "She always was a liar." "This proves the divorce was all her fault." If you like to dump on your ex-wife, it puts your children in a difficult position. They won't like to hear her abused and they'll often feel forced to cover for her. Children love both parents and don't like to hear Dad attack Mom, or vice versa. If they try to defend her, they'll be afraid you'll yell at them for it. So they may back off and not dare talk to you at all.

Prying for information. You want to know what your ex is up to, so you pump your child for information. This is something I know all about—I did it often. I hardly ever came right out and asked straight questions; I usually asked oblique questions. Instead of bluntly asking my son, "Does Mommy eat out a lot?" I'd ask him, "Where do you go when you eat out with Mommy?" Or, instead of "Is your Mom still dating Oscar?" I'd say "Your Mom's still dating the same guy? What the heck is his name?" And so on. And looking back on it, I can see that at the time, I thought Christopher didn't know what I was doing. But of course he did. Or at least he sensed it. He sensed I was up to *something*. And I'm sure it couldn't have helped but make him uneasy and unhappy.

"Tell Mom that . . ." It's easy to use children as messengers between you and their mother. Too easy. Asking them to carry verbal messages—or even written notes—sets the stage for problems. First, they can easily garble a message and deliver the wrong information to her. Second, it puts them on the receiving end of a lot of emotional undercurrents from both you and your ex. Here's an example.

You (to child): "Tell that mother of yours that . . ."

Her (to child): "Oh, your father said that, did he? Well, my lawyer will straighten this out!"

The child knows that both parents are angry, and he hates to be in the middle. Also, he may irrationally blame himself for your anger or believe that he in some way is the cause of it.

Discussing your ex in your child's presence. If your child is with you when you talk about your ex with your friends or family, he'll hear everything you say (even if you've put him in the other room!). And if there's the least bit of sourness in your voice as you mention your ex, he'll pick up on it—and feel uncomfortable.

Listening to the kids talk about Mom. Whenever the children are with you, you'll inevitably hear a certain amount of talk about her. Even if they know—or suspect—that you don't get along with her and don't want to hear about her, they'll slip often and mention her in conversation. It may be hard for you, at times like these, to let the talk roll off your back. You may flare up with comments like, "Oh, she said that, did she?" or "What on earth is she thinking of?" or "Is she crazy?" or "Honestly, I don't know why anybody puts up with that woman." It's up to you to keep your comments to yourself, even if the kids can't.

The "mother trick." This is one that *she* plays on the kids. She'll call you one day and say, "The kids are driving me crazy. I need a rest. You take them for a while." So you agree to pick up the kids. Then, when she's delivering them to you at the door, she says to them, "Oh, I'm going to miss you so much. You're going away and leaving your poor Mommy all alone." This is terribly unfair to the kids. It throws a lot of guilt on them for "leaving" her. She won't take responsibility for her own feelings, so she throws it off onto them. What can you do about it? Nothing at the time. You just have to grit your teeth and make bland comments. To admonish her in front of the children would be adding insult to injury. The only thing you can do is call her later when the children won't hear you and ask her not to pull that stunt again.

Therapy can work wonders for children if they're going through a difficult period. Just to get outside the Mom-and-Dad framework of their lives for an hour a week may make all the difference. The tension and turmoil between the two parents is magnified in the children's eyes, and what Mom and Dad consider to be just ordinary give-and-take may appear to a child to be out-and-out warfare. This takes its toll on the child's mental and emotional equilibrium. Often it's more uncomfortable for them as helpless observers than it is for you as an active participant.

Just remember how uncomfortable you were when your parents quarreled in your presence (even if they thought they were having nothing but a "discussion"), and you'll know how your own children feel now.

My son's therapist helped him admit to the hurt he was feeling when he got caught in the middle between me and his Mom. Chris rapidly got very wise to the situation, and he became the one who often alerted me when I got a bit too steamed up over my ex-wife. When I'd unconsciously start letting myself talk about her in his presence or perhaps try to probe him for information about her, he'd often say bluntly, "Dad, I'd rather not talk about Mommy here." Talk about a cold shower! But, frankly, he was right, and the blunt comment was just what I needed.

Three Thorny Situations

Special events. It's your teenage daughter's graduation—your son's championship baseball game—your young daughter's ballet recital—the school play—parents' day at camp. These are events both you and your ex will probably want to attend. And therein lies a problem. What do you do if you're going through a difficult period and you don't want to see her? You're determined to go; she's determined to go—but neither of you wants the other to be there.

Well, first let's hope that the situation isn't quite as bad as you make it out to be. You may hate the sight of her, but, truthfully, will you fly into a rage if you merely get one glimpse of her across a crowded auditorium? If you can swallow the idea of at least being in the same room with her, then you've got a base to work from.

It won't do any good to try to convince your ex that she shouldn't attend the event. ("This is a baseball game, and I'm the coach. I can't see why on earth you want to go.") It's totally unfair, and she probably won't listen anyway. And don't let *her* try to argue *you* into staying away. ("You never attended school meetings before. Why don't you just stay away?") Both of you have a right to be in attendance. To argue otherwise is silly and pointless, since neither of you will listen to the other's reasons anyway.

If you're really determined not to run the chance of bumping into your wife, then maybe you can do some fancy sidestepping on scheduling. If it's parents' day at the children's camp, for instance, maybe you could go in the morning, your ex in the afternoon. If it's a baseball game, she might attend the first half, you the second. These are unsatisfactory compromises, it's true, and you can't expect your children to be happy with them. But if this is the only way you and she can work things out, then so be it: it's better than not attending at all.

If it's a case of continuing events, like baseball games or school plays, you may be able to alternate your appearances. You attend this week, she attends next week.

Once you've told the children you'll attend, don't chicken out. No person in the world is so disappointed and let down as a child whose parent fails to show up at a really important event he has promised to attend. No matter how much you dislike meeting their mother, no matter how many second thoughts you may be having about the wisdom of going to the event, once you've promised your child, be there no matter what.

And last but not least, you should have a contingency plan in mind for coping with the thing you're trying most to avoid: having to talk to your ex-wife. This does happen. You're in a crowd at the baseball game and you turn around—and there she is. Or she's with friends and they insist on dragging her up to you. What then? It pays to make a plan in advance so you're not taken by surprise. The easiest way is to nod hello and make an immediate excuse to get away. "I was just going to help Jimmie with his costume." "I promised Nancy I wouldn't be a minute." And then skedaddle. This may be rather rude, but it's better than running the risk of starting to hiss or trade insults. The most unpleasant situation is when you are with friends who don't know your ex and you are forced to introduce them. The only way to get through this ordeal with any kind of grace is to murmur something like, "Have you met my son's mother?" or "This is Caroline Meyers, my daughter's mother." And then trot out one of your all-purpose excuses and beat a hasty retreat.

Tantrums. If you and your ex are on bad terms, the children may hear her say a lot of bad things about you. She may succeed in painting such a bad picture of you that the children start to hate or fear you. Tantrums come next: "I hate you!" "You're awful!" "You're mean and cruel and you hurt Mommy."

You'll see red. The irresistible temptation may be to start yelling back at them. "I'll wring that woman's neck!" "How dare you say you hate me. I'm your father." "You're such an idiot, you can't see how she's poisoned your mind against me."

A friend of mine went through such hair-raising scenes for two months following his divorce, and he told me that the only way he succeeded in controlling the problem was to block the words his children said and concentrate on the simple fact that they were angry. He told me, "I had to treat them as ordinary tantrums, as if the children were complaining about having to go to bed too early or not being allowed to have another piece of candy. If I paid attention to *what* they were saying, I always seemed to get as mad as they were, which only made matters worse. I discovered it was best not to listen to the actual words but just to go for the anger. I'd say, 'You're really angry. I'll bet you feel pretty miserable,' or 'Tell me more about what's bugging you.' "

Which seems like excellent advice. If you take the children's tantrums in stride, they'll begin to calm down and see that you plainly are not the monster your wife says you are. If you start screaming at them, though, you'll only reinforce the picture she's given them of you.

And by the way, if it's any consolation, you should be thankful that they still trust you enough to express difficult emotions in your presence, even if they do take the form of a tantrum. It's better than silence and fear. It's a lingering sign of confidence in you— another reason why you should go easy on the child when he or she has a screaming spell.

Your ex keeps the children from you. No matter what it says in the separation agreement about visitation rights or shared custody, it sometimes happens that the mother will try to monopolize the children and keep them from seeing their father.

"Oh, hello, Hank. You want to talk to Little John? I'm sorry, but he's busy, he can't come to the phone right now."

"I know it's your weekend to see the children, but they don't want to see you. There's nothing I can do about it."

"Hank? I'm sorry to call like this at the last minute, but Susie's got the flu and she won't be able to visit you this weekend."

Newly separated fathers always worry that this is going to happen to them, but luckily it doesn't happen nearly as often as they fear. And if it does happen, it's often only a "phase" their ex-wife is going through and it disappears after a couple of months. All of which indicates that you shouldn't get too upset or fly off the handle if it happens to you. If you fight your ex-wife tooth and nail, the problem will only get worse; but if you play it cool, it will *probably* get better. (It's like what I learned at the karate classes I took at the police academy. You pull back when your opponent pushes; you don't follow the typical reaction of returning blow for blow.)

Meanwhile, how do you cope? Single fathers who've been through it say the best way is to keep cool. Don't accuse your ex-wife point-blank of keeping the children from you. After all, if she says they're too sick to visit you, she may be telling the truth. Even if you know she's lying, a subtle campaign is best. If, for instance, she sometimes keeps you from talking to the children on the phone, just keep calling on your normal schedule, or more often; sooner or later, she'll run out of excuses. If she won't let them visit you on Thanksgiving, then say you'll take them for Christmas instead and send her a letter confirming the fact so it'll be hard for her to back out of the arrangement later. If she sometimes cancels your visits by saying the children don't want to see you, then next time you *do* see them, have a friend take pictures of you and the children together, smiling and having fun. Give copies to the children. Let your ex see them. It'll be harder next time for her to say, "But they don't like to visit you."

Her Male Friends

Sooner or later, she'll have a lover. And you'll hear about it. Oh, will you hear about it! Your friends will tell you all about it (friends love to be the bearers of bad news). You'll know more than you ever wanted to know about the new person in your ex's bed.

Even if your friends mind their own business and clam up on the subject, you'll hear about the new man from your children. "We went to the zoo with Mom and Larry last week." "Dad, Larry's taller than you are." "Larry made blueberry pancakes for us last Saturday for breakfast. Why don't you make blueberry pancakes, Dad?"

We all go through it. I don't think there's a single father alive who hasn't had to grit his teeth and get used to the idea of his children's mother having a lover. Of course, if she originally left you for another man, then you've already gotten used to it. But even if *you* left *her*, and she was heartbroken, eventually she'll get over it and find somebody new. And that's when the psychological shit hits the fan.

No matter how much you may have wanted to get rid of your wife, no matter now much you disliked her, you were the main man in her life. In the most primitive sense, she was *yours*. You knew her, in both the biblical sense and the ordinary sense.

And so when she gets a new main man in her life, you're assaulted by a swarm of conflicting emotions. Jealousy, for one ("She's screwing someone else"). Anger, for another ("How dare she flaunt this guy in front of me"). Hurt, for a third ("I've been replaced"). Fear, for a fourth and last ("He's going to take my children away from me").

Ten to one, you'll begin competing with Mr. New. Even if you've never laid eyes on him, you'll still feel you're in a contest with him. We all do it. We want to prove to ourselves that we're better men than our ex-wives' new boyfriends. If we can prove *that*, it doesn't hurt so much to know she has someone else. After all, if he's a poorer lover, a poorer father, a poorer man in general, then we can just shrug him off contemptuously. "Alicia went from me to him? Poor woman. Really, I almost feel sorry for her."

But doubts keep cropping up. *Is* he a poorer lover? a poorer father? a poorer man? Maybe, just maybe (and this is what none of us likes to admit to ourselves), he's the better man. Maybe he's got us beat. It's this ugly little suspicion in the bottom of our minds that causes all the problems when our ex-wives take up with new men.

The bad news is that there's not a hell of a lot to do about this. Nothing but the passage of time will take away the trauma. But, even so, there are one or two tricks that can take the sting out of the situation, at least until you've been able to get used to it.

For instance, if you're angry at being replaced by another man and at being compared (perhaps unfavorably) to him, try looking at the flip side of the situation: *he* is being compared to *you*. And he doesn't like it any better than you do. If anything, he likes it less. If the children say to you, "Larry's taller than you are," you can be sure that they're also saying to Larry, "My dad has bigger shoulders than you do." Comparisons work both ways. When you're mad at being compared to him, just think how he's gritting his teeth at being compared to you. And, frankly, you're in the stronger position. He'll always be "Mom's friend" or "Uncle Larry," but you'll always be "Dad."

If you're jealous, the only trick that works is to keep yourself in the dark about the guy. As we said in the last chapter, ignorance is bliss.

And if you fear that the man will usurp the children's affections, there are no real tricks. Just don't overreact. *Nobody* can replace you with the children. As you've told them often enough, they're yours for life, and you are theirs. This is simply a fact. The children won't question it. The problem is all in your mind, not in theirs. They'll simply treat the guy as a new friend, not as a new father. It's up to you to see him in the same light. You don't have to change your style with the children, you don't have to go overboard with treats and affection in an effort to "win back" their affection. You never lost it in the first place, and you never will.

Competition, envy, and resentment of another man in your children's lives is just another way of getting down on yourself, another way of tying a ball and chain to yourself. It's all too easy to cater to a negative self-image. Deciding to see yourself as a worthwhile person is the challenge that's worth taking.

Money

All your dealings with your ex-wife come down to two things in the end: the children, and money. We've mentioned children; now let's talk about money.

In meetings with single-father groups, I hear relatively standard complaints about money. My friend Louise, who is a coordinator for women's support groups, says she hears a similar chorus of complaints from women, except that they're exact mirror images of men's complaints.

MEN

"She's a leech. No matter how much I pay, it's never enough."

"She uneconomical. She's a lousy manager of money."

"She spends money frivolously."

"She has more money than I do."

WOMEN

"He's stingy. He doesn't give me enough to live on."

"He expects me to pay for all my expenses on one lousy little check a month. I'm not a miracle worker."

"I've got to have *some* amusements. I'm not a robot. He wants me to live like a nun."

"He has more money than I do."

From my own experience with fathers, I can say that, all other things being equal, the divorced father doesn't object too strenuously to paying alimony and child support, even if the size of the payments seems awfully big to him (and it always does!). He recognizes that he has an obligation to support his ex-wife and the children, and he accepts the obligation. But—and here's the crux of the problem—all other things are not always equal. And it's when something goes askew with the established relationship that the problem of nonpayment is likely to crop up.

There's really only one basic reason a man actually stops paying alimony and child support: he feels he is being systematically cut out of his children's lives. Single fathers don't like to feel they're being made fools of or that their ex's are milking them for all they're worth and giving nothing in return. As one nonpayer explained, "If she doesn't live up to her end of the bargain, I won't live up to mine. So when she starts withholding the children from me, making excuses to cancel my weekend visits, and bad-mouthing me to them all the time, that's when I say to myself, 'Okay, I'm not going to pay.'"

It's when men feel they're being frozen out of their children's lives that they fight back with the only weapon they've got: turning off the money spigot. Which is unfortunate, since nonpayment solves nothing. It's a completely unsatisfactory solution for both the man and the woman. She doesn't get any money, and he doesn't get the children. Neither of them gets anything positive out of the situation. They're both worse off than they were before.

Almost every single father I know says he would much rather pay the monthly checks and have access to his children than not pay and not have access.

If you use money as a weapon against your wife, then you're playing a losing game, no matter how much you may enjoy putting her in a financial bind. You're backing yourself into a worse corner, since it's inevitable that your relationship with your children will suffer.

To avoid this no-win situation, it's worth a lot of effort to try to settle money disagreements before they get so out of hand that you begin to consider nonpayment. When money problems are concerned, a stitch in time saves nine. Which brings us to the Third Law of Dealing with Ex-Wives:

Rule #3: Be up front about money.

Being up front about money means *talking* about money disagreements instead of just stewing over them in silence. Alas, most of us would rather stew than get together with our ex-wives and really hash out the problems. It's simply easier to sit there and grumble, "So she thinks she's going to take all my money and then not let me see the children, does she? Well, I'll show her."

Ten to one, she means nothing of the kind. Or perhaps she's just seeing how much she can get away with. It's much better to confront her and discuss the situation than to let it escalate until you're both too far apart to negotiate. Chances are you can work things out.

Money problems come in all shapes and sizes. There are others besides the nonpayment one:

She gets a job (or a promotion) and earns more than she was earning before. You feel she should agree to a reduction in alimony, but she never mentions it, and she goes on accepting your monthly checks.

She moves in with her boyfriend (or he moves in with her). Her expenses go down, since he's helping pay the rent. You feel she should volunteer to take less money from you.

She has some unexpected expenses and asks you to help her out.

You want to spend some extra money on the children (sending them to camp for the summer, for instance). You feel your ex-wife should share these expenses with you, but she makes no move to contribute a penny.

In all these situations, you can either get mad and say to yourself, "Well, if she wants to play dirty, I can play that game as well as she can," or you call her up and make an appointment to get together to discuss the problem.

Please try the second alternative. In nine instances out of ten, it'll make you a lot happier in the long run.

You'll be nervous about it. Money problems always make anybody nervous. So follow a reassuring step-by-step procedure.

1. Make an appointment. Don't just call her on the phone any old time and try to discuss it informally. It's better to be business-like and a bit "official" about it, since you're both bound to be uneasy with the subject.

2. Don't assume the worst about her. Be open-minded and let her have her say. She's probably *not* out to defraud you and empty your pockets; she's probably just taking the path of least resistance. For instance, if she's gotten a new job and is earning twice what she used to earn, and she's still accepting your alimony and child-support payments, you may be tempted to think, "This is a con job! She doesn't need the money. She's trying to take me to the cleaners!" Well, probably she isn't. She may just keep cashing your checks because that's what she has always done, and it's easier to go right on doing it than to rock the boat. Besides, if you don't make a protest, she may assume you don't mind.

3. Don't make accusations. For one thing, they may not be true. For another, they'll only make it harder for you to compromise. Politeness usually pays. Concentrate on yourself without pointing a finger at her. "I'm worried that the children haven't been able to see me lately, and sometimes I get so upset I feel like not sending the child support checks." "Now that Jeff has moved in with you and is contributing to your expenses, I think it would be fair if I

made a reduction in my alimony checks." "I'm willing to help you pay for your classes, if you feel you really need them, but I also feel I should get some other concession in return."

4. Compromise. Be prepared to accept a less-than-ideal settlement in the interests of solving the problem quickly without a lot of tears and bad feelings. After all, any change in the situation is better than what you had before.

5. Put it in writing. You don't need a twenty-page contract drafted by lawyers, but at least write out the bare bones of your agreement in simple language for each of you to sign.

The period of the separation itself is usually the hardest. With the passage of time—and with the divorce itself—things tend to quiet down, and your relationship with your ex-wife settles into a more comfortable equilibrium.

It's all a question of getting past your anger and arriving at a workable level of respect, trust, and mutual support.

For a long time after I separated from my wife, I assumed that respect in separation was impossible, or a myth dreamed up by goody-goody counselors. But this all changed one weekend when my son and I visited friends of mine at their house in the country. It was a weekend made for disaster, or so I thought. My friends were separated and hadn't lived together for some time. But here they were, together for the weekend, the wife with her new male friend, the husband with his new female friend. And their two children were there, too.

I expected fireworks, but there wasn't a sign of discord all weekend. The two ex-spouses treated each other with absolutely genuine respect. Even though they were very different in temperament, they respected each other's differentness and never let themselves get drawn into disagreements. Neither did they take advantage of each other's vulnerablility, though this would have been very easy, since each of them still had unhealed wounds from the separation. And, hardest of all, they listened to each other, without judgment and without interruption. Everyone had a good time, even the two children, which to me was an infallible sign that there were no unpleasant emotional undertones anywhere.

That weekend opened my eyes. It was a big incentive to improve my relations with my own ex-wife. If *they* could do it, *I* could do it. Linda and I got together soon after that and ended up talking for four hours—the first time since our separation that we'd been able to sustain such a long communication. It was also the first time I'd simply talked and listened to her, without also wanting to get something out of her.

It was the beginning of a mutual but businesslike respect for each other that eventually became the norm in our relationship. It led to a kind of mutual support system where our son was concerned. If Chris got into a disagreement with his mother and called me on the phone complaining or in tears, I would listen to him pour out his story, but at the end, I'd tell him that he'd have to work out the problem with his mother. And Linda would do the same for me if the tables were turned.

We became a team again, albeit a team who lived apart, not just two strangers who happened to be called Mom and Dad.

6.

THE OPPOSITE SEX

Married men are secretly envious of separated fathers. They may not admit they're envious, but they are. They regard separated men as having regained the long-lost days of bachelorhood, and the realization makes them a bit itchy with their comfortable but domesticated lives as married men. They conveniently forget the pain that separated men go through and fantasize instead about the kid-in-the-candy-store sex lives that the newly single man is supposedly indulging in.

There may be an element of truth in this view, but it's far from the whole truth. Separated men do undoubtedly go on sex sprees, but for every day spent in the great sexual supermarket of modern life, there's another day spent in the loneliness and misery of being separated.

The only sure thing you can say about the single father's life is that it's *un*sure. Chaos is often the order of the day. One day he's a swinging bachelor on the loose, a wolf prowling the tempting sheep herds of available women. The next he's a depressed loner who wants only to be mothered.

And this is not just some passing phase, either. It doesn't evaporate in a week, or even a month. This crazy period goes on for *months*. It may be six months or a year before the single father begins to settle down and regain his equilibrium. It's not at all the enviable existence that married men may suspect it is.

Having been through all this, I can vouch for the fact that it's full of confusion and contradictions. In regard to women, I found that after my separation, I had three absolutely conflicting reactions to them:

I hated them—they reminded me of my wife.

I needed them—they offered comfort and caring.

I used them—they were handy sex objects to play with.

These feelings didn't occur with willful intent. I was just lost, needy, and confused—and along they came! As I've since found out, they're all utterly standard reactions for the newly separated man. The first feelings, right after the separation, are likely to be misery, loneliness, and a sense of loss. After these abate a bit, a sex spree often comes along. There's nothing like a parade of women to soothe a case of wounded vanity and hurt feelings. It really bolsters the old masculine pride. And, frankly, it's so easy these days, when women seem to be as eager for it as men. There's nothing to stop us from having a new woman every night, if that's what we want—and believe me, there are times when that's exactly what we want.

Sex is a great catch-all for other needs and emotions, which is one reason it gets such a big play from aching separated men. When you're hurting from your separation, it's awfully gratifying to be close to another human being . . . to be hugged . . . to be able to express yourself without holding back . . . to be rid of loneliness for a while . . . to discharge your emotions. Sex is usually the only activity that lets you do all these things. It's hard to come right out and say to someone, "I feel bad and I want to be hugged," but under the cover of sex, you get the hugging without admitting what you're really asking for.

Sex sprees come and go, and they don't really solve anything except your hormonal imbalances. They're temporary Band-Aids for your wounded heart, they stanch the bleeding for a while, but they don't cure the disease. In between sprees, it's back to uncertainty and confusion. There's no telling in what direction your mood will veer. You may fall into a gloomy antisocial depression when you don't want to see women at all—or on the other hand, you may rush headlong into a new marriage.

Whatever sort of relationship with women you have, you'll tend to be touchy and suspicious. This comes out in several ways.

You may feel women want too much of you or are pushing too hard for "commitment" (which is often the last thing you want after your separation).

You may feel (or suspect) that a woman is manipulating you, "using" you for power or money.

You resent how much money you're spending on women. Not many of them want to go Dutch treat. And money is inevitably the one thing you don't have enough of during your separation.

Your *real* relationships with women begin after you've gotten through this period of turmoil. Until that's behind your back, things will be difficult. When you're in the middle of this schizoid emotional state, you may think it'll never end. It *will* end, however.

Reassuring Truth: No matter how messy things may seem, they do straighten themselves out with time. It may take a year (or even longer—who knows?), but you will eventually become your old self again.

Or a better self. That's the real thing to hope for. In my own case, for instance, after the sex sprees and the emotional pig-outs were over, I found I was gradually becoming able to admit to my real wants and needs instead of gratifying them surreptitiously under the cover of sex—the need to be touched, to be hugged, to be listened to, to be open, to be cared about.

How Women View Separated Men

As separated fathers, we're usually so busy thinking about ourselves that we don't have any time left over to think about our female friends. We may neither know nor care what's going on in their heads. But any relationship is bound to be easier and more productive if you know where the other party is coming from, and it's the same with women. A woman's view of you is often completely different from your view of yourself. I learned some of this through experience, and I also heard some from female friends.

—Some women will be attracted to you *because* you're a father. That is, they'll assume you're caring, steady, and reliable, in a word, domesticated—not one of those good-time charlies who have no ties in the world and live by a strict love-'em-and-leave-'em philosophy. This kind of woman will find your fatherhood attractive and will assume you are basically Mr. Good Guy.

A woman can learn a lot about you by observing how you act with your child. Do you listen? Are you patient? Are you demonstrative? Do you treat the child as a person in his own right? Do you give the child "space"? Are you kind? Are you compassionate? Observing you with your child gives her a sort of advance early warning of your emotional makeup.

—Some women will distrust you for being a father. Far from being reassured by your state, they'll be put off. This woman usually has "nest-building" instincts and a strong wish for a family of her own. She may suspect that because you have kids already, you don't want any more. You've got all the family you need; you don't need another one. So she'll avoid you in favor of men with no progeny.

—"He's just using me." Any kind of woman can make this complaint, and most of them do at one time or another. Frankly, the complaint is often justified. The woman feels that the man is just using her for sex, which in fact is all too often exactly what he's doing.

—"He talks my ear off." Women make this complaint often, though men don't realize it, because the woman won't always come right out and say it to them. It happens most often in the early stages of separation, when you may use her (perhaps without realizing it) as a sort of crying towel, giving her the whole history of your marriage, complaining about how poorly your wife treated you, attempting to prove that the separation isn't your fault, in general trying to talk out your misery because talking makes you feel better. Alas, she is rarely so entranced as you are.

—"He thinks I'm his mother." Some women may enjoy the mother role, but the majority don't. If you telephone a woman too often on the spur of the moment when you're feeling blue, or get in the habit of leaning on her for favors, or pouring out all your troubles to her and expecting a lot of sympathy and soothing words in return, she may feel you're treating her like a comfy but sexless mom rather than as a woman in her own right.

—"He's afraid of commitment." This is women's most common complaint about single fathers. Most women are looking for a serious relationship (even if they don't come right out and say so), and commitment may be the last thing on *your* mind. In fact, your situation makes you extraordinarily sensitive to the signals a woman gives off. The minute you detect that she's pushing a little too hard; or trying to get "under your skin"; or asking too often or too eagerly, "When will I see you again?"; warning bells go off in your head. You'll pull back, or cut off the relationship entirely. This is a good thing in the long run—you're not ready for commitment yet—but to the woman, it will of course look as though you are just another shallow, exploitative male chauvinist pig.

(By the way, this sort of pulling back is not limited to men. Some women, even though they consciously want an exclusive commitment, may unconsciously have a need to stay free.)

The Remarriage Trap, or, Out of the Frying Pan and into the Fire

In the ups and downs and ins and outs of your relationships with women, there will inevitably be times when the wheel comes full circle and you long for marriage. It usually happens when you're feeling lonely, frightened, helpless, and frustrated. It's especially virulent if you've never really lived alone before and don't know how to conduct life as a solitary person. You may feel you'll go out of your mind if you have to face another night alone in a double bed . . . eat another TV dinner . . . put on another pair of dirty socks in the morning because you haven't done your laundry lately . . . leave for work without breakfast because there's no one to prepare it for you.

You're a perfect set-up for the remarriage trap. You want a companion so badly that you marry the first halfway eligible woman who comes along. And you often marry on the spur of the moment, without giving yourself time to live with the idea for a few weeks or months before taking the plunge.

WARNING: Don't Do It!

Don't remarry too soon. Remarriage itself is fine, as long as you do it for the right reasons. But I don't know *one* of these marriageson-the-rebound that has lasted. Almost all of them end in divorce sooner or later—usually sooner. As soon as the initial euphoria wears off, the new groom finds that the new marriage is no different from his old marriage, and it's headed for the same rocky end. It's a case of the old proverb: He who forgets the past is condemned to relive it.

Before remarrying, you've got to face yourself and deal with the reasons your marriage broke up in the first place. If you forget how unsatisfactory your first marriage was, your second usually won't be any better. It takes time to remedy—or at least to admit—the faults and undefined needs in yourself that led to the breakup. And until you've given yourself that time, remarriage is always going to be dangerous.

(Incidentally, a good book on this subject is one written for women, *Loving Men for All the Right Reasons,* by Dr. Bonnie Maslin and Dr. Yehuda Nir. It has a lot to say about how we tend to be influenced by our unconscious neurotic needs, which often push us into a steady succession of unsuccessful relationships. It's a good book to read before remarrying.)

Women's Reactions to Your Marital State

A problem: women are sensitive to the nuances of marital status, and if you tell a woman the "wrong" thing about yourself, she may drop you like a hot potato. This is fine for her—she's gotten fair warning and abandoned ship without too much wear and tear on her heartstrings—but it's emphatically not okay for you as you stand there steaming with frustration.

Telling lies about yourself so as to be more attractive to women is, to use a good old Victorian word, dastardly. But I've done it, you've done it, we've all done it—and we'll go on doing it. If you're looking to get "something for nothing" from a woman, then you'll often be tempted to lie about yourself. But I'd recommend telling the truth, for the simple reason that it helps you *be yourself.* Then the woman can take it or leave it.

Here are the usual lines that women hear from separated men:
—"I'm separated." The literal truth about you. Unfortunately, it often has a deadly effect on women. It means you're still married,

in the technical sense. And as long as you are still married, there's no chance for *her* to marry you. Even if she only wants a brief fling, she may feel you're somehow taking advantage of her; it looks like you're trying to have your cake and eat it too.

—"I'm divorced." It's fine to say this if it's true. But sooner or later, every single father uses it as a substitute for "I'm separated" because it doesn't carry that odious implication that you're still married. There are a million ways to "justify" this little white lie—e.g., "I'm divorced in spirit"; "My marriage is really over in every important way"; "By the time she finds out I told a lie, I really *will* be divorced." But no matter what you say, it's still a lie, and if she does find out, she'll be annoyed.

—"I'm single." The big lie. This is really unfair to the woman. But we all say it at one time or another. What can I tell you? Save it for the singles bars when you know it's only going to be a one-night stand.

—"I have children." This *may* be a turn-off to a woman if she's strictly a playgirl. But even if she only wants a quick, no-obligations fling, the fact that you're a father probably won't turn her off. As long as she likes *you*, then the existence of your children probably won't mean much to her (unless, of course, you force them on her, in which case she'll rightfully have a gripe). I'd say from experience that most women like the fact that a man has children —it's attractive, it gives him an aura of maturity and masculinity that can be a definite aphrodisiac.

And incidentally, you'll find that divorced women are usually more sympathetic to you than single women are. Divorced women have been through it themselves and know you're a fellow spirit.

Children and Women

If your children are with you for substantial periods of time, they'll meet your women friends as a matter of course. There's almost no way to avoid it. But if you're a weekend father or a long-distance father, then your children and your female friends need not meet. And they *won't* meet until and unless you want them to.

Most men prefer to keep women and children separate, all

things considered. It's easier that way. There are two very good reasons not to introduce all your women friends to your children:

You may simply have too many women. To show children a constant parade of women through your life is confusing to them and may give them an idea of your emotional life that you'd rather not convey.

You're courting trouble with their mother. If she hears about your women, she may be goaded into one of the standard responses: "I won't let the children visit you and be exposed to that life-style." "Keep your 'lady friends' away from my children." "Forget about seeing the children—I won't have them exposed to such immorality." Nine times out of ten, these responses really have little to do with the children and are actually only your ex's way of saying, "I'm angry that you left me and now you're running after other women." But why tempt fate? As long as she has custody of the children, it just doesn't make sense to inflame her and give her an excuse to keep the children away from you.

And the children themselves may prefer not to meet your women friends. They can be just as insistent on having you to themselves. They can get jealous very quickly if they think a woman is monopolizing you or competing for your affection or taking you away from them. After a separation, children are especially sensitive about their relationship with you. The separation has given them a shock; they may perceive it as a kind of rejection. So they'll be doubly on the lookout for any further threats to their stability. They may get cranky or silent if you bring women friends along on occasions that are supposed to be "family" events. And they can get very hurt or angry if they sense you're spending more time with a woman than with them.

Children in general aren't very interested in their parents' friends. An introduction to a woman will be, at best, a rather dull social obligation for which they have to put on "company manners."

In practice, you'll often be spared the decision of whether to introduce your women friends to your children. Many single women (never married) will prefer not to meet your children.

They'd rather not have any competition for your time and attention—or they're afraid they'll be awkward with the children and won't know what to do—or they fear they'll be a negative influence on the children—or they simply don't want to be bothered. There's no point in trying to force your children on them. Be grateful they're keeping matters simple for you.

EXCEPTION: Divorced women will usually be willing, even eager, to meet your children. And at the same time they're usually much better with children than single women, since they've had experience in marriage themselves.

The most livable way to handle the matter of introductions is this: don't introduce a woman to your children unless you're relatively serious about her.

But once a woman has become a friend or you are in some way getting close to her, then by all means do introduce her. Don't hold back because you want to "spare" the children. There's nothing wrong with female company as long as there's not too much of it. And it's a good thing for the children to learn that though you may have other people in your life who are close to you, that doesn't mean you're going to abandon *them*. It takes time and practice for children to learn this.

The actual introduction will go smoothly if it's handled as casually as possible. The worst possible introduction I can think of is something like this: "Kids, this is June. She's going to be your new mother." This is much too abrupt and much too late. The children should have met June long before there was any hint of remarriage. She should have been presented to them in a much more low-key manner. And she *won't* be their new mother—they still have one.

The best introduction is one that would do equally well for a man as for a woman. Just as you might introduce a male friend to your children by saying, "This is Jim. We're on our way to play handball," you can introduce a woman with something equally casual, such as, "This is Susan. We're going to the movies," or "This is Margaret—she's in my tennis class."

There are no emotional overtones to these introductions. They won't make the children suspicious. Words like *girlfriend, dating, close,* and *relationship* are best kept out of introductions. For the same reason, don't say, "Louise has been wanting to meet you," or "I want you to meet Louise." That implies an emotion on your part or hers, and the children will sense it. Not that there's anything wrong with emotion—it just should come later. There is no need to include it in a simple introduction.

The future doesn't have to be mentioned, either. "You'll be seeing a lot of Kimberly from now on." "Joan wants to get to know you real well." "I know you children and Annie are going to be good friends." These statements may all be true, but the children may translate them as: "This woman is pushing her way into our lives, and our dad is trying to force her on us." The future will inevitably bring enough jealousies and frictions of its own. Don't court them any sooner than necessary.

Women Overnight

Should women stay with you overnight when your children are with you?

If you have your children only on weekends, it's easier to keep women and children separate. There isn't time for so much heavy "relating" on a two-day weekend. Everyone will feel short-changed—the children, the woman, and you yourself. You'll probably all appreciate it better if you save the weekends for the children alone and see *her* during the week.

But if you have your children full-time or for long periods at a time (two weeks, a month, six months), then you'll have a hard time avoiding overnight guests. You can't go to her place *all* the time.

Everyone will slide into the situation more easily if you treat it casually. Don't make a big thing of it the first time a woman stays overnight with you. Don't say any more than you need to say. Which is: "Fran is going to stay overnight with me tonight." Or even better: "Fran is going to stay overnight with *us* tonight."

That's all that needs to be said. Don't be embarrassed. Don't offer long explanations. Don't mention sex. There's an interesting thing about children that I've discovered: if they're under twelve, they often won't connect "staying over" with sex. No matter how precocious they may seem to be, they often don't grasp sexual connections that you may think are obvious. They can *talk* sex, but they may not understand how and when it is actually taking place. Having had no experience of the act, they lack the perspective for visualizing it in others. So when your lover stays overnight with you, it may simply not occur to them that sex is the object of the visit (or one of the objects of the visit). In their minds' eye, they'll visualize "closeness" or "friendliness" rather than "sex." And they'll often simply assume that your female friends are staying over with you the same way they stay over with *their* friends.

Once my son and I were watching a TV movie together in which a young woman had to vacate her apartment for a night and went to stay with a male acquaintance of hers. When the man tried to jump into the bed with her, she said, "What do you think you're doing?", and he had to sleep on the sofa all night. My son was young at the time, and I wondered how this scene was affecting him. After the show was over, I asked him how he liked it. He said the part about the bed didn't make sense. "Here's this guy letting the woman stay in his apartment. So why couldn't he sleep in his own bed? Why should she kick him out? It didn't make sense." The idea that sexual motives were involved had bypassed him completely.

When a woman does spend the night with you, you can avoid awkward hitches by observing a few sensible precautions:

—Watch your language. Children are all ears. Keep the talk aboveboard—no sly sex talk between you and her.

—No nudity (except in your bedroom behind the closed door). Strange naked women in the house won't exactly help your children's peace of mind.

—No private jokes. The children will feel left out.

—If possible, the woman should leave before the children get up. This avoids complications. But there are plenty of exceptions to this rule. Sometimes it will be understood that your friend (especially if she's a long-standing friend) will stay for breakfast or for the whole day. In that case, there's usually little problem. But the first time the children meet a woman friend of yours, it does help if her appearance is kept short and sweet.

Teaching Children Discretion

Among your various women friends and/or sex partners, you're bound to run into complications. At times, you'll go overboard in the lady department and feel like an inept juggler trying to keep too many oranges in the air at once. It's bad enough trying to keep the various women apart, or trying to remember exactly what you have told each one. But it's even worse when you have to factor the children into the equation.

A friend of mine was once dating several women at the same time. It wasn't the most comfortable situation, because the women were aware of each other and they weren't too happy about having to share the man. The mess hit the fan one day when one of his friends (Lisa) called my friend, and his son (Luke) answered the phone.

LISA: "Hello, Luke. Is your father there?"

LUKE: "No, he's not here. He's out with Mary Lou."

Lisa, to put it mildly, was not pleased. It took my friend weeks to straighten out that situation.

Obviously, if you're going to get involved with women, it helps if the children are taught discretion. You don't want them answering the phone and saying, "Oh, just a minute. Daddy's in the bedroom with Tanya. I'll get him," or remarking to your mother-in-law, "We had a good time when Millie stayed overnight with Daddy."

You won't be able to avoid all these gaffes, but you can forestall a lot of them. If your children don't already know that there is a difference between what is public in life and what is private, you can explain that there are some things that are to be kept strictly within the family. And a little guidance in phone discretion is always helpful: "When anybody calls, here's what you do—just take the name and don't give out any information."

Whether to Remarry

Most single fathers want to remarry—eventually. And as long as they avoid the too-hasty remarriage (out of the frying pan and into the fire), there's a good chance that the second marriage will be much more successful than the first. But at the same time, the single father will find a lot of questions standing in the way of a new marriage:

Is it what I really want?

How will the kids react?

Should I marry to provide a mother for the kids?

Does my fiancée know why I'm really marrying her?

If the second marriage is to be successful, all parties should be clear in their minds about how it's going to affect them.

What YOU Must Know

Basically, you must know *why* you're getting married. This sounds simple-minded, but it's surprising how many single fathers go into a remarriage without fully knowing why they're doing it. First and foremost, the marriage must satisfy *your* wants. Leave everybody else out of it—the children, your fiancée, your relatives, and so on. If you can honestly say that the marriage will satisfy *you*, then it's the right thing to do. You'll have to be realistic, even slightly hard-hearted, about the children when you ask yourself this question. They may not be so eager for the marriage as you are. They may have some trouble accepting a new woman in their lives on a formal basis. Here's where we get down to the nitty-gritty. You'll have to recognize that your needs are different from theirs. Don't sell yourself short. If the marriage is really what you want, don't back out of it because you're afraid of how it'll affect the kids. The kids will get used to it. On the bottom line, it's a question of who will suffer more—the children (if you do get married) or you (if you don't).

What THE WOMAN Must Know

She must know that you are choosing *her*, for herself alone, because you love her. If she suspects, even a little, that you're marrying just to provide a mother for the children, the marriage will be off to a shaky start. And if *you* suspect you're marrying to provide a mother for the kids, you shouldn't be getting married at all. It's better to break an engagement than to marry for the wrong reasons.

What THE CHILDREN Must Know

They must know that no matter whom you marry, the woman won't come between you and them. They must know that they are yours forever. Tell them this bluntly, and keep telling them. They must know that nothing she can do will change your affection and love for them. If they feel this in their bones, with no reservations, it will make the marriage much smoother and will forestall envy or resentment of your new wife.

As in all your interactions with your children, the secret is communication. The lines of communication between you and them must always be open, so that your messages come through loud and clear and so that their feelings never have to be suppressed or concealed. In fact, it's not a bad idea actually to ask your children what they think of the woman you're getting serious about. Let them tell you, honestly and fully. If they do have any reservations, you might as well know them now and begin to deal with them. And then again, their perspective on the woman may be both surprising and enlightening, and you'll really learn something from them.

If the children become jealous or disturbed by the new woman in your life, let them know that this is normal and neither shameful nor punishable. Encourage them to admit their feelings to you—in private. The point is not to admonish them or lecture them but simply to let them talk. Anything you can do to encourage them to talk is good. They need to communicate fully on the subject. Glossing things over won't help. Let them know that *feelings* are not *problems,* and that just because they have certain feelings about your woman friend does not mean that they've done anything bad. The one essential is to keep the lines of communication open, so that the children can talk to you about how they feel. Some jealousy on their part is normal and to be expected, and often one good long outburst will discharge their bad feelings.

If your future intended has children of her own, a certain amount of friction will also probably develop among the children of the two spouses. Stepfamilies are another area in which the single father has not had prior experience. Education helps. Prepare yourself ahead of time by joining a stepparent support group, or touch base with a family counselor. This will get your new marriage off on a more rational and better equipped basis than your first one.

7.

SEPARATION AND YOUR JOB

When I first separated from my wife, my job was both a godsend and a pain in the ass: a godsend because it distracted me from my problems and forced me to think about something else for eight hours a day; a pain in the ass because sometimes there were days when I felt so overwhelmed I couldn't stand the nuisance of having to go to work.

If this sounds contradictory, it was. It just goes to show how mixed up and confused my reactions were at the time. In the long run, my job was a lifesaver. It provided something for me to focus on outside my personal life. But in the short run, there were those days—not a whole lot of them, but enough—when the job was really hateful, when I was too depressed to concentrate on work, sometimes too depressed to go to work at all.

I've since learned that this reaction is common with single fathers. For me, it all worked out in the end, finally. After I'd been separated for a while, things settled down; my job slipped back into its old perspective and I stopped having those roller-coaster changes of feeling about it.

Then I had to face the second main problem that all single fathers have with their jobs: conflicts between job and children. It's the old familiar *Kramer-vs.-Kramer* situation of the father not having time for his work and his children, too.

This problem, unlike the earlier one of being depressed on the job, hasn't gone away. I am still occasionally plagued by it, and it'll always be with me, at least until I stop working or my son gets old enough to leave home (neither of which is right around the corner).

Depression on the Job

Some men hardly feel a twinge of emotion after their separation. They're the lucky (and rare) ones. They go to their jobs every morning without a care in the world and continue to function as well as ever. For the rest of us, though, it's not so easy. It's hard to force yourself to go to work when you're feeling miserable, depressed, or exhausted. I know from experience that there are times when you think you'll go out of your mind if you have to go to work and put in those damned eight hours. And even if you do pull yourself together and get out the front door in the morning, you feel so gloomy or preoccupied on the job that you can hardly force yourself to do any work.

There's no instant way to avoid feeling depressed. Sad but true. And, what's worse, when you are depressed, there's no easy cure.

But there is one saving grace in the whole situation: you're probably not actually depressed about your *job* (even if you think you are); you're depressed about your life in general. This may sound like a picky or pointless distinction, but I don't think it is. When you wake up in the morning and say to yourself, "I can't stand the idea of going to work today," what you're really saying is simply, "I'm just plain miserable." It helps to separate the two, so that it doesn't seem as if every aspect of your life has gone to the dogs.

So if you're going to be miserable anyway, you might as well go to work and be miserable there.

Actually, it's usually not as bad as this. This is the "worst case" situation. Most of the time, work is really the best antidote to misery or depression, no matter how unpleasant it seems. You have to look at the flip side of the coin: going to work forces you to be active, to get out of bed in the morning, to move, to see other people. It's better than staying home alone, moping, as the hours drag by. Even if you can't concentrate at work and feel you're just going through the motions, it's better than doing nothing.

Almost always, it's best to go to work, no matter how little you feel like it. The job will get your blood flowing, take you out of yourself.

You may go through one or two really bad periods—anywhere from a day to a week or two—during which you really think you can't stand to go to work. Even if you're prepared to do something drastic like take your vacation days in order to stay home, I recommend you drag yourself to work.

The problem with staying home from work—or pampering yourself in any other way—is that this can lead to addictions of various kinds. Separated men are dangerously prone to getting hooked on anything that gives them relief from their pain. Alcohol, drugs, food, cigarettes—these are the most common. But slacking off at work is another, and if you get into the habit of calling in sick (or taking long lunch hours or anything else), it tends to snowball into an addiction. I used to think it was a good idea to pamper yourself when you needed it, but I have changed my opinion. I used to pamper myself, in my worst periods of depression, with Haagen-Dazs ice cream, but after a few days of that, I began to get fat. It was better not to pamper myself at all—just to suffer through the bad periods.

It comes down to this in the end: if you're well enough to think and to feel, you're well enough to go to work. Even if your thinking takes the form of endless miserable rehashings of your breakup, and even if your feeling is nothing more than one big ache about your current situation, you should still go to work. You're well enough to function; you *are* functioning when you're thinking and feeling.

Children Versus Job

If you have your children on more than just a weekend visitation basis, you're going to have conflicts with your job. This applies to shared custody or any other arrangement in which you have them for weeks or months at a time. The basic problem is that you don't have time for both children and job, so both suffer.

How children suffer:

They see you for only a few hours every evening (if that).

You have trouble getting them to school on time in the morning.
You're not at home when they are.
If you work overtime, you hardly see them at all.
Often there's no adult in the house when they are there.

How your job suffers:
You're often late in the morning.
You sometimes have to take time off to attend to your children's needs.
You may have to give up lucrative overtime in order to be with your children.
You may be interrupted a lot at work by having to talk to your children on the phone.

The problems tend to be at their worst toward the beginning of the separation period. For one thing, you're likely to be feeling less than your best, so your job may suffer from your inattention. For another, your living situation is unsettled (especially if you've just moved), so you waste a lot of time running errands and attending to other nuisances. Most important of all, your children are going through a traumatic time of their own and they'll be most difficult to manage, and need more love and attention from you than usual.

Most books I've read about single parenting have a standard piece of advice for this situation: you have to decide which is more important, your children or your job. I've always thought this was a pretty useless piece of advice, frankly. It certainly never helped me. My son and my job were *both* important. Most of us just don't have the luxury of choosing between one and the other. Presumably we're supposed to say something like, "My children are the most important thing in my life; therefore, I'm going to quit my job so I can spend more time with them." Can anybody really do this? It's just plain impossible.

Of course, the problem is never quite as clear-cut as this, but the basic principles are the same. For instance, you decide you want to spend more time with your children. This means you'll have to give up some of your overtime, or stop putting in those occasional late hours at the office. But that overtime and those late hours are how you support the children. If you give them up, it's they who'll suffer. It's a no-win situation.

It always comes down to money. If you've got plenty of money, you won't have any trouble. If you don't have plenty of money, you're stuck.

Well, almost.

There are some ways you can resolve the children-vs.-job conflict, or at least make a dent in it. None of them is perfect, but frankly they're the best we can do under the circumstances.

BEST WAY: Get help. Getting help can mean anything from hiring a full-time housekeeper to getting a baby-sitter once a week . . . from sending your children to an expensive day-care center to dropping them off at your mother's for the day.

You may say, "But I want to spend *more* time with my children. If I hire a housekeeper or send them to a day-care center, I'll have to work longer to pay for it, and then I'll be seeing *less* of them." This may or may not be true, when you come right down to it. You may be worried unnecessarily. Take an example. If you hire someone to clean your apartment, it may actually free you to spend more time with your children, since you won't have to do the work yourself. (You can't do much with your children when you're jockeying a vacuum cleaner.) Of course, you'll have to pay the cleaner, and that may mean having to work an extra hour or two a week. But you'll probably find that the hours you lose in overtime are more than compensated for in hours of free time gained with your children. Which is the whole point.

Even modest help can mean a lot. If you worry about not being at home when the children return from school, hire a baby-sitter or a neighbor for those two or three crucial hours every afternoon when you're not there. If you have a cleaning person, try to arrange his or her hours so that they coincide with when you want someone in the house.

Young children (under five) are a bigger problem. They cannot be left alone, anytime. You'll simply have to bite the bullet and resign yourself to finding someone to take care of them when you're at work. The arrangement you make depends on how much money you can spend. If you're flush, you can send the children to a fancy day-care center. If you're not quite so rich, you can still find nuts-and-bolts day-care centers within your range. If you're definitely on a budget, day-care centers will probably be too expensive. In that case, your best bet is probably another single parent who'll take care of your children for a reasonable fee. Some single people make a business of this, and it's cheaper than day care. You can also explore cooperative child care, in which each parent donates a certain amount of time on a rotating schedule. If you're more or less broke, then your parents may be your last resort (if they live relatively close to you)—they may be willing to take the children during the day.

Incidentally, some corporations and businesses are beginning to offer day-care facilities on their premises. If you can tap into such an arrangement, you're really in luck. These day-care centers are usually so inexpensive (compared to others) that it's worth a lot of effort to find one or to petition your employer for one, if there isn't one.

And always check with other single parents to see how they manage. You never know what smart moves they may have thought up. Don't know any single parents? Then join a single-parent support group.

NEXT BEST WAY: Work at home. This may not be possible for most of us, alas, but if your job allows it, certainly give it a try. Employers are getting a lot more flexible about this. Even one day a week at home can make a big difference. But make sure you can actually get the work done at home. It's no use working at home if you're going to be distracted by children all the time.

THIRD BEST WAY: Move. Most single fathers, no matter what their job is or how many children they have, possess one problem in common: they spend a lot of time going back and forth—back and forth between home and job, back and forth between home and school, back and forth between home and Mom's. Any hours you can salvage from this thankless round of schlepping is time saved to be with your children. If you have shared custody, it pays to live close to your children's mother. You never have to spend time picking up the children and delivering them. You don't have the nuisance of packing. The children can just walk or bike from one home to the other.

Another alternative is to move closer to the children's school or (if they are young) day-care center. This cuts out lots of transportation time. Or even move near your parents. Then press your mother or father into service as a "volunteer" baby-sitter. The last possibility is to live close to your job. Commuting time is wasted time. So if you can cut down on your commute, you can be at home longer with the children.

These are the three best ways I know to cut down on problems caused by friction between the demands of your job and the needs of your children.

8.

WEEKEND FATHER

You've left your wife . . . you've moved to a place of your own . . . you and your wife have agreed the children will be with you on the weekends . . . you're wondering how you'll adapt to this new regimen. And right in the middle of this situation sits one big fat fear like a rock in your gut that won't go away: "The children will forget about me. Two days a week isn't enough. They won't remember I'm their father. They won't love me anymore."

Terrifying. It strikes right where it hurts the most—your identity as a father. For if your children forget you, then you're not a father anymore. To lose a wife may not be so bad, but to lose the children would be devastating. (Just stop for a moment and admit to yourself those words that males are always supposed to hide: "I'm very scared.")

This fear may be so bad that we don't dare admit it to ourselves. But it's there, all right. It's always there. And so without realizing it, we'll do *anything* to prevent losing our children's affection.

Enter the sugar daddy.

The Sugar Daddy Syndrome

If you only see your children on weekends, you want to make every minute with them count. This is the "quality time" concept that every divorced man has heard about. In the absence of "quantity" (and with today's custody system, few of us ever feel we have enough time with our children), then "quality" is all that's left to us. Quality can't fully make up for quantity, but we've got to make the most of it. At one time or another, we've all gotten fired up about the idea and said, "Okay, I'm going to make my time with the children really *count*."

It sounds easy enough, but it isn't. Quality time is one of those concepts that's hard to pin down and apply to real life. When you really stop and think about it, what is quality time, anyway?

Let's say right here, without further ado, that quality time is not what many of us think it is. The ideal weekend with your children is not—repeat *not*—one in which you ferry them around to the zoo, the mall, the movie theater, the local McDonald's—and spend the rest of the time with them rooted in front of the boob tube (in this case, the boob is not the tube—it's you).

If you spend the weekend entertaining the children, you're being a sugar daddy, not a father. Every separated man goes through the phase sooner or later. Already shaken by the separation and/or divorce, he gets even more shaken by not having unlimited access to his children. And so he tries to compensate. Terrified that his children have forgotten—or will forget—him, he tries to cram a week's worth of living into a weekend. He lavishes the children with money and attention like Santa Claus on some particularly festive Christmas Eve or like maiden aunt Janice at her twice-yearly visit. If the children want pizza and ice cream for dinner, then that's what they have. If they want to go to the movies on Saturday afternoon, then Dad dutifully trundles them off to the theater, even if he had actually intended to do something else. If they insist on sitting glued to the television set while Dad slaves over dinner in the kitchen, Dad doesn't question it; he just rolls up his sleeves and goes back to peeling the potatoes. He doesn't dare discipline the children when they're bad, for fear they'll sulk. He doesn't even like to disagree with their opinions when they're talking about something completely inconsequential over a meal. Anything to keep the children happy. He buys them gifts, toys, doodads—practically anything they ask for, if he can possibly afford it—and then returns them to their mother Sunday night thinking, "There. That was a weekend they'll never forget. They had a ball. They can't forget their poor old Dad after a weekend like *that!*"

Well, they *can* forget. And they do. The sugar-daddy routine works like gangbusters for a few weeks or a few months, but then things change. The children get restless and distant. They begin to be bored with Dad. They treat him with the same kind of easygoing contempt they would have for an overindulgent grandfather or jolly uncle whose principal function is to provide amusement. Dad in his turn gets anxious or even bored as the sugar seems to be running low.

It all comes down to the oldest cliché in the book: money can't buy love. And that's exactly what the sugar daddy is trying to do—buy his children's love. He's bribing them with money, indulgence, and attention. But money, indulgence, and attention won't buy affection. They'll just establish him as an easy touch. When he buys the children toys, thinking, "They'll think of me whenever they play with this," he's deluding himself. They won't think of him—they'll simply forget. Children don't have long memories. The sugar daddy ceases to be "Dad" and becomes simply a kind of genial robot dispensing gifts.

Quality time doesn't consist of playing the sugar daddy. It consists of simply being there for your children—being there in the fullest possible sense—in really being yourself, the *real* you, so the children understand you're still their father, that you haven't changed into a strange new person just because you're not living with their mother anymore. As usual, this takes time and patience.

Getting Off on the Right Foot

The easiest way to get out of the sugar-daddy syndrome is not to get into it in the first place.

Life as a single father begins the day you move out (or the day your wife moves out, if that's the way it happens). That's also the day you should, ideally, begin to set the pattern of your future relationship with your children.

You'll feel guilty about leaving. That's natural. That, added to the inevitable insecurity you'll feel about things in general, is the source of the sugar daddy. If you can conquer the guilt and the insecurity, then you probably won't fall into the sugar-daddy syndrome. Conquering guilt and insecurity is easier said than done, but you can make a good try by reminding yourself constantly of two things:

1. You're still their father. No matter what happens—no matter how far away you may be, or how little you may see them—no matter what you may say to them—you are still their father. You will always be their father. Nothing can change this fact. There is no substitute for father love.

2. They'll still love you. The children won't stop loving you when you move out. They love both their parents, and a separation won't change this fact. They may be angry—there will probably be tears, tantrums, and accusations—but this doesn't mean they don't love you. On the contrary, it's an indication that they do love you and are hurting because of the separation. You don't have to buy back their love, since you've never lost it.

If you can drum these two points into your head, you won't be so fearful about losing your children's affection or being forgotten by them. You can go about being your old self without worrying that the children will reject you.

Being your old self is the essence of avoiding the sugar-daddy trap. Presumably you weren't a sugar daddy while you were still with your wife, and you don't have to be one now that you're separated.

Translated into practical terms, avoiding a sugar-daddy role means letting your children know that when they are with you, things are going to be the same as they were before. You're not going to be a new person, and they're not going to behave differently with you. Your home is going to be a real home, not a sort of weekend motel. When they're with you, they're going to be at home, not "on vacation" or "just visiting." They'll see you as a normal everyday person whose life has obligations and routines much like their own. Give them as much of yourself as if you were still living with them full-time. Even if you're going through a period of personal change or transition, show them *that*. You don't have to go so far as to burden them with embarrassing confessions or unfair loads of adult responsibility, but by the same token, don't try to conceal everything under the falsely jolly mask of the sugar daddy. In other words, be human. They will still love you.

I've already mentioned (in Chapter 1) some of the ways to get off on the right foot when you separate. I don't mind harping on them, since I think they're important.

Starting Right

—Show your children where you live, right at the beginning. They need to know you have a home. When they're away from you, they like to have a mental image of where you live.

—Reassure them that you're getting along okay, that you have a place to sleep, that you have enough to eat. This means really *show* them: point out the bed; open the refrigerator.

—Give them territory of their own. "Whenever you're here, this room . . . closet . . . drawer . . . will be yours."

—Involve them in the arrangement of your home. "Where do you like this picture—over the couch or between the bookcases?"

—Have some things from your old home that they'll recognize, for the sake of continuity—an armchair, a chest of drawers, some pictures.

—Make sure they have your phone number, preferably in a personal "address book" of their own.

If you haven't gotten off on the right foot—and have fallen into the role of the sugar daddy—it's not quite so easy to get out again. You'll have to do some backtracking. It won't do any good to try to change your spots overnight. This will only confuse and discombobulate the children. They'll wonder what's gotten into you. If they've become accustomed to you lavishing them with attention and gifts, they certainly won't appreciate it if you suddenly start acting like a drill sergeant with a platoon of unruly recruits. You have to go about it more circumspectly.

How Not to Be a Sugar Daddy,
or
Seven Commandments for the Weekend Father

1. You are not a servant. You're not there to wait on them hand and foot. Your role in life is to be their father, not their man-servant. Therefore, don't let them run all over you. Don't let them

get away with murder. When they overstep the proper bounds, discipline them just as you always have.

2. You don't have to keep them occupied every minute. You're not a social director at a holiday resort for bored young people. Nowhere is it written that you have to provide a constant round of entertainment for them, taking them from the movies to McDonald's, from the game arcade to the zoo, from one friend's house to another's, from Friday afternoon until Sunday night.

Children actually soon grow weary of weekends like this. You can see it in their air of inattention and fretfulness and peevishness. They need some time to themselves. And even if there are times when they do get bored, it's not the end of the world. Kids with two parents in their home get bored sometimes, too. Let them know that there will probably be some free time every weekend in which they'll have to entertain themselves, as well as some time when they'll have to give you a hand with the household tasks.

3. Establish a routine. Children should have some general guidelines of what to expect when they're with you. A routine (not too rigid, though) helps. For instance, on Friday night: pickup and dinner at your place. Saturday morning: TV. Saturday afternoon: sports or an outing. Saturday night: dinner out. Sunday: free time plus dinner that you all prepare together. Or whatever. A totally unstructured weekend is too conducive to the resort hotel mentality that goes along with being a sugar daddy.

4. Establish continuity. The children's weekends with you should be linked with some thread in their minds, so that your life together is not just a series of disconnected outings. For instance, you could work on a big project with one (or all) of the children—building a boat . . . building a tree house . . . painting a mural on the walls of the bedroom—something that would take weeks or months. Or buy a dog that the children would look forward to seeing on their visits. Arrange for your daughter to have her music lessons or for your son to have his pottery lesson on the weekend, while they're with you. And then, beyond that, remember what the children talked about this weekend so you can mention it next weekend. "What ever happened to Mary Lou last week after she

swallowed the bubble gum?" "What did your class think of the picture of the giraffe we took at the zoo?" "Does your teacher have the cast off her broken leg yet?" This makes for a sense of continuity from one weekend to the next.

5. Assign responsibilities. If you're not going to be a social director, then the children will have to do some of the household work while they're with you. There's no reason why they shouldn't, and, unless you get into the habit of being a sugar daddy, they'll expect to help out, because that's what they do at Mom's. You don't have to be a martinet about it, but let them know that there are certain tasks to be done that you need help with. In general, they'll prefer to do something different at your place from what they do at Mom's. For instance, if your son washes the dishes at Mom's, then let him set the table at your place, or take the cleaning to the laundry. The children will appreciate the variety. They'll also appreciate responsibilities that are challenging to their age. Let the fourteen-year-old go out and do the shopping for you instead of just doing the dishes.

6. Involve the children in real-life activities. Their time with you shouldn't be one long holiday with no relation to everyday existence. When they're with you, they should know that they're continuing the same kind of life they lead on weekdays and that they're definitely not simply on vacation. One of the best ways to do this is to let them see that *you* are not on vacation, either. Bring home some work to finish up over the weekend—take the children to the office with you on Saturday to pick up the mail—let them accompany you to the bank to deposit your paycheck—anything that will let them see you in a real-world role. By the same token, you can encourage them to bring some of their work with them for the weekend. For instance, if you're good at math, they can bring along their math homework for you to check.

7. Don't bargain. One of the worst consequences of slipping into a sugar-daddy role is that you end up bargaining with the children. After all, this is what the sugar daddy is basically all about—he's making an implicit bargain to buy the children's affection. The advanced stages of sugar daddydom lead to naked bribes. "We'll go to the movies tonight because you're being so nice to Daddy."

"If you stop crying, I'll take you to Kentucky Fried Chicken." "I'll buy you a bike if you'll come here for Thanksgiving."

While you shouldn't bargain, there's nothing wrong with an occasional honest compromise. "Yes, you can watch an extra hour of TV tomorrow, but in return you'll have to wash the dishes after dinner." It's only when you're nakedly bargaining for love—rather than simply for help or cooperation or an exchange of favors—that the situation gets out of hand.

Painless Pickups

—Have a definite schedule. Let it be understood that you'll pick up the kids every Friday afternoon at four, for example. And then stick to it. This avoids complications. It's also reassuring to the children, especially the younger ones.

—If you're going to be late, phone the children's mother to let her (and them) know. This not only prevents friction with her, it also lets the kids know that you *will* be there and that you care enough about them to call. (If possible, talk to them as well as to their mother.)

—If the kids aren't ready when you arrive, don't complain or make a scene. Help them get ready, if you can do so without making it seem as though you're indirectly criticizing their mom. Save your objections for a later private phone call to her. If it's the kids' fault that they're not ready—if they're just plain lazy or slow—deal with them yourself, later.

—Don't insist on being "boss" the minute you arrive at their mother's place, even if the kids are "legally" yours as of four o'clock. You're on her territory, and it's only common politeness to defer to her. If you feel she's stalling intentionally, call her later privately to complain, and if necessary to make some other arrangement so it doesn't happen again.

—Don't get into a talk with her. If you have any issues to discuss with her, don't discuss them now. Save them for a private meeting when the children aren't present.

—Don't hang around. As soon as the children have their coats on, leave.

—See that the children pack neatly for their return. They should check to make sure they're not leaving any clothes behind. And don't let them mix up the clean clothes with the dirty ones in their suitcases.

—If the children are nervous about getting back on time and want you to rush to leave, don't get peeved and snap at them. Be neutral and calm. If you can arrange a later return time for next week, then do so privately with their mother. Otherwise get them back *early*—they'll be less likely to press you again another time if they've seen that the return to Mom's isn't a race against the clock.

The Zoo Syndrome (and How to Avoid It)

Go to any movie in which one of the characters is a single parent and you'll inevitably see a scene in which Dad (or Mom) takes the children to the zoo on Saturday. I don't know why it is, but people just seem to assume that zoo-going is as inevitable a part of single parenting as getting the children to eat their vegetables or telling them to brush their teeth.

But those movies do have a point: too many fathers fall back on ritualized weekend activities like going to the zoo, instead of doing things that are more truly interesting to them and their kids.

The zoo is interesting once, or maybe twice. But you can't go there every weekend. If you do, you'll all get bored. It's silly to go week after week simply because you think it's the thing to do and because you don't bother to arrange anything else to do.

The zoo is usually the last resort of the weekend father who is desperately afraid of the children being bored. He provides a whirlwind of activities for them, hoping to keep them occupied and amused. The zoo, the movies, fast-food restaurants—any activity at all, in fact—eventually grows stale because it is *just* amusement—diversion and nothing more. A weekend of diversions sooner or later goes stale on the children.

What children really want are activities they can participate in. Going to the zoo doesn't quite qualify. It's looking, not doing. The same applies to all the other zoo-type amusements that single fathers turn to in their attempts to avoid any "air space" in the weekend.

The ideal weekend is one that includes a variety of activities, not just amusements.

something old: to provide reassuring routine and a sense of continuity in life

something new: to provide spice and variety

something active: to let off steam

something quiet: to provide a time for privacy or for talk, and to give a sense of real life and "ordinariness"

Young children in particular need the reassurance of routine, and they'll appreciate having at least one activity that they do every weekend—anything from going to the local hamburger joint on Saturday night to taking the dog to the park on Sunday afternoon. They'll tend to resist new activities at first ("Aw, Dad, do we have to?"), simply because they are unfamiliar with them. But this is no reason to abandon them. They'll usually get interested in the new activity as soon as they are actually doing it.

Older children don't have such a strong need for routine. Doing the same thing every weekend will drive them out of their minds. One routine activity is quite enough, say, a family meal on Sunday night. As for the rest of the weekend, they need less structure than younger children.

There will be times when the activity you have planned just doesn't click with the children. The fishing trip bores them to distraction . . . the hike makes them cranky . . . the shopping expedition leaves them cold. You've got to expect this to happen at least once in a while. Children can't be expected to have equal enthusiasm for all activities. While it's okay to insist gently that they try out the activities you suggest, it's not necessary to force the activity through to its grim conclusion if you can see that it isn't working out. It's like spinach—you have a right to ask the children to at least taste it, but if they don't like it, what's the point in forcing it on them? Let them eat broccoli instead. So when you see that your Saturday afternoon activity is plainly a mistake, the best thing to do is simply abort it. Go home and do something else. You'll save a lot of wear and tear on your nerves by doing it this way. Don't apologize for having dragged the children into the activity; just withdraw gracefully and go on to something else.

With children over six especially, you can compromise or have a system of trade-offs. With my own son, for instance, we take turns calling the shots on activities. I'll join him for a horror movie, and next time he'll rough it with me at the handball court.

Cooking:
Weekend Activities

If you're not a total klutz in the kitchen, then cooking is one of the best weekend activities. It's down-to-earth and "real," and it can also be fun. For some reason, lots of fathers, the first time they get into the kitchen with their kids, think they should make something sweet and gooey, like fudge. Forget it. Fudge (or any kind of candy) is boring to make—an eternity of mixing and stirring—and then you have to wait hours while it hardens. Children lose interest; they get distracted. They like recipes from which they can see quick results. They think in terms of now, not later.

If you're an experienced cook, you won't have trouble finding more than enough recipes for children to get involved in. If you're not an experienced cook, then you may be interested in the results of a poll I've been taking over the years. I've asked single fathers what their children's favorites are. Here are the results.

Four kinds of food children like to make most:

1. flaming dishes
2. popcorn
3. decorated cookies
4. Chinese egg-drop soup

It may look like an odd list at first sight, but it's not really hard to see why children like these foods: they're all fast and simple, and they give exciting results. They have the added advantage that even young children can cope with them. It doesn't require any great dexterity or concentration to pour a beaten egg into a pot of soup, or to sprinkle colored sugar on cookie dough. Not that you'll necessarily let your four-year-old flame the steak. That's a task for the older child—but a child of any age will love to watch the flames.

Flaming Dishes

Lots of dishes can be flamed, and it takes only 45 seconds.

Heat liquor in a small pan for a moment until it begins to bubble or fizz around the edges. Then take it off the heat and light it with a match. Pour it over the dish just before you serve it.

A quarter-cup of liquor is usually plenty. Don't stick your nose right into the pan when you light the alcohol—the flames can singe your eyelashes. Or if you want to use less alcohol, just sprinkle a little liquor directly onto the food and ignite it immediately (don't give it time to soak in or it won't light). No need to worry about the children getting tipsy; almost all the alcohol will burn off before the flames die.

A few dishes that can be flamed:

MEAT

(use brandy or cognac)

steak (or broiled hamburgers)

fried pork chops

liver

broiled chicken

ham (sliced or whole, baked or fried)

DESSERTS

(use brandy, cognac, or rum)

baked apples

fruit cake

apple pie or tart (warm, not cold)

baked Alaska

Chinese Egg-Drop Soup

This is an easy recipe, even easier than popcorn. It's also unusual and spectacular in its way. When the beaten eggs are poured (or "dropped," as the Chinese say) into the boiling soup, they form long, interesting threads and strands. Children are fascinated.

I've made this recipe with my son since he was six years old. I'd be the chef, and he'd be my helper. I'd open the can of broth, he'd pour it into the pot. I'd crack the eggs; he'd pour them into the soup. I'd regulate the gas, he'd stir the soup. We got it down to quite a routine. I got into the habit of giving him the empty eggshell after I'd cracked the egg and saying, "Here, ditch this." As he got older, I began to let him do more of the preparation. Then came the day when he cracked his first egg, and, without even thinking about it, handed me the shell and said, "Here, ditch this." We had a good laugh about that.

To make egg-drop soup for two people, open a can of chicken broth (a 13³/4 oz. can) and heat it to a boil in a pan. Crack two eggs into a dish and beat them with a fork for ten seconds or so. Turn the heat off under the boiling broth and pour the beaten eggs into it. Stir the eggs around in the broth a few times.

And there you are. That's all there is to it.

If you want to be fancy, you can add a chopped-up scallion (both the white and the green part) to the broth while it heats.

Getting Children to Talk

The most infuriating thing that can happen to a father is to look forward to a weekend with his children and then find that they have nothing to say.

"How are things at school?"   "Fine."

"Are you having a good time in your club?"   "Yeah."

"How are the dancing lessons coming along?"   "Okay."

"What's on your mind?"   "Nothing."

Of course, he knows the child does have things on his mind, and he wants to know what they are. But a weekend—two short days—often isn't enough time for the child to relax and get back into the groove with Dad. Ergo, no talk.

Children won't talk unless the atmosphere is conducive to talk. This often takes some clever maneuvering on your part.

The first thing to do, as I've mentioned before, is remember what the child talked about *last* weekend. Trivial topics are fine—his clothes, his friend who broke his arm, the kite-flying competition at school, the neighbor's cat who couldn't get down from the roof. Bring up these topics as soon as you see the child. Also, make a point of remembering the names of his friends and his teachers at school, and mention *them*. When you bring up these old familiar subjects on Friday night, they'll create a familiar atmosphere that will help the child loosen up.

Children will often tend to be more talkative when they're in the midst of an activity. When you're trying to get your child to open up, try playing checkers with him, or going to the laundry, or going fishing—any activity you're both familiar with and that doesn't require a lot of mental concentration. It's much easier to get a child talking by easing him into a routine activity than by sitting him down portentiously and saying, "All right, let's have a talk." Even the most lackluster chitchat during an activity will usually lead eventually to the subjects that are really on the child's mind.

If a routine activity doesn't work, try a strenuous physical activity—jogging, handball, squash, or something else equally rigorous. Hard physical activity tends to get the child's defenses down. Some children have an easier time revealing what's on their minds —or just chitchatting about ordinary daily affairs—when they're puffing and panting in the midst of a demanding workout.

For young children, you may have to provide an indirect opening. Ask the child to draw a picture, and then talk about it (the picture will often tend to reveal what the child is thinking about). Or ask a "fun" question, such as, "If you could be king over your friends for a day, what would you do?" or "If you were the teacher at school . . ." or "If you could go anywhere you wanted to right now, where would it be?" One man I know gets good results with, "If your dog could talk, what do you think he'd be saying now?" These questions get the child going. After he or she is talking, you have no trouble. It's getting the child started that's difficult.

9.

LONG-DISTANCE FATHER

I'll begin this chapter with the confession that I've never actually been a long-distance father myself. Linda and I have always shared our son between us, and since we live in the same city, I've never had to face the problem of him going away to another city or state to live. Of course, I *felt* like a long-distance father the summer Chris went away to camp for two months. That two months dragged out to an eternity. But the whole point of him going to camp was to let him be on his own, away from me and his mother. Most long-distance fathers are in just the opposite situation—their biggest concern is to stay in close touch with their absent children.

But though I haven't been a real long-distance father myself, I've got plenty of friends who have been.

CARL . . . moved to New York after his divorce, and his ex-wife remarried and moved to California. He lost touch with his three children for the next two years, until they suddenly decided to spend one summer with him. It was a big readjustment for him, but now he keeps in touch with them religiously in California.

BOB . . . was relocated to the East a year after his divorce, while his daughter remained in Kansas with her mother. Bob calls his daughter every Sunday and sends lots of letters. He provides her airfare back East for a two-week visit every year and for holidays whenever they can be arranged.

LOU . . . started out as a weekend father and then became a long-distance father when his ex-wife married again and moved to

Oregon. He frankly hated the idea of being separated from his children by the width of a continent, but he wasn't willing to give up his job and move west to be near them. He and his ex-wife had to work out a new custody arrangement so that Lou could have the children for several weeklong or monthlong periods during the year.

FREDDY . . . has always been a long-distance father. His wife moved out of the house with the children and went to her parents, two hundred miles away. She has since moved even farther from Freddy. Freddy's not rich and can't afford trips to see the children. He only sees them once a year, on Christmas or Thanksgiving, when they visit his parents for the holiday.

ANDREW . . . started off living in the same city with his son's mother. They had joint custody of their son, who spent an equal amount of time with each parent. When the mother changed jobs and relocated to the South, that arrangement had to be completely revamped. Now their son lives with Andrew during the school year and spends the summer with his mother.

Among them, these men have evolved a battery of ways to keep in touch with their absent children. Most of this chapter is derived from their experience.

Facing the Realities

Long-distance fathers don't usually set out to be long-distance fathers. Something comes along after the separation that puts a big physical distance between them and their families. It's almost always one of the following:

He gets a job in a distant city and has to move.

His ex-wife gets a job in a distant city and has to move.

His ex-wife can't stand him and moves to another location to get away from him. ("I'll move so far away you'll never see me—or the kids—again, you creep!")

But though the long-distance father didn't ask to be separated from his children, he is separated from them, and he has to live with the fact and make the best of it. This can be done, as long as he recognizes and accepts the realities of his situation.

Almost any long-distance father will tell you that the first thing you must recognize—the First Rule of Long-Distance Fathering, so to speak—is this:

To have any success as a long-distance father, you've got to be on reasonably good terms with your ex-wife.

If your wife has left you and moved to Oregon, taking the children with her, she can (if she wants to) stifle all your attempts to keep in touch with them. She can tell you the children are out when you call. She can discourage them from writing to you. And so on and so on.

So you've got to have your ex-wife on your side. The essential point about long-distance fathering is that you want to have access to your children—if not actual physical access, at least access by phone and mail. And when the children are with your ex-wife—whether it's all year round or six months per year or whatever—she controls that access. So you've got to cultivate a good relationship with her or you'll be out in the cold as far as fathering goes.

The other thing you have to accept, assuming you're on a relatively friendly basis with your ex, is that you're not going to be the dominant influence in your kids' lives. When you were still married, you were the big boss. You had the biggest say (or at least an equal say) in how your children were going to be raised. Now, as a long-distance father, you're not going to have that influence. You won't be there to discipline them . . . to tell them to brush their teeth . . . to help with their homework . . . to make sure they eat right . . . to keep an eye on the people they associate with. Their mother will now be the one to do all these things.

I've known single fathers who refused to accept this situation and who would grit their teeth and say, "It's not going to happen to me—I'm not going to give up my hold on the kids." And then they'd burn up the telephone wires with constant calls to the distant family in an absolutely futile attempt to maintain their old authority.

But it never worked. In parenting, there's no substitute for proximity. If you're not there, you simply can't exert a strong everyday influence.

Which is not to say that you'll be powerless. Just because you lose your everyday influence doesn't mean you have no influence at all. The situation is much as if you'd sent the children to boarding school: you may not see much of them, but you're still their father. You are still recognized as an authority figure in the family. And it's taken for granted that you have a say in all important matters.

There's no voice that can take the place of a father's voice, and that voice is crucial to children. Don't forget this. There's no substitute for your love, and even if you feel discouraged by the distance between you and your children, hang in there: *they need you.*

Making It Work

Once you're clear about what your new role will be, you can go about forging the new relationship with your kids.

Whenever I talk to experienced long-distance fathers, I always find that the point they emphasize most is not how often they phone their children, or what they say in their letters, or how they negotiate with their ex-wives over the kids' vacation time, but rather the importance of establishing routine and continuity in their relationship with their children. These seem to be the two magic words: *routine* and *continuity.* The most successful long-distance father I know says, "You've got to establish a clear routine with your children, and you've got to stick to it. It doesn't matter so much how often you call them but that you call regularly on a specific schedule. If you call only once in a while, when the mood strikes you, and only write letters when you feel like it, you might as well give up being a father at all."

If your children know that come hell or high water, you'll call them every Sunday night, then they'll know they can depend on you. And you'll remain a real "presence" to them, even though you don't see them often in the flesh.

The only problem with phone calls is that children have a limited attention span and get distracted easily, and routine calls can be dull and uninformative.

YOU: "How's everything?"

CHILD: "Fine."

YOU: "School okay?"

CHILD: "Yeah."

YOU: "What did you do today?"

CHILD: "Nothing much."

Conversations like this drive the long-distance father crazy. Often he imagines the child is lying or holding back something, but this usually isn't the case. It's just that in their terms, the children are giving perfectly accurate answers to the questions.

The real problem is not that children give inadequate answers, it's that fathers ask inadequate questions.

The best way to get children to really talk is to be specific in your questions—specific but not demanding. Instead of vaguely asking, "How's school?" be more specific and say, "How are things working out with the new math teacher?" or "What class is most fun this year?" or "Do your teachers give you a lot of homework?" Instead of "What've you been doing?" ask about a specific interest or hobby. "How did the baseball game against Oshkosh go?" or "How's the dog?" or "Have you taught your brother to use the personal computer yet?"

I remember a piece of advice my high school English teacher gave. He called it the First Rule of Conversation:

Don't ask questions that can be answered yes or no.

This is especially pertinent with children. Questions that require only yes or no for an answer put an end to conversation. They don't get a conversation flowing. Children will take you at your word and think that all you want is a monosyllabic answer. If a question can possibly be answered yes or no, a child will answer it yes or no. They won't understand that you want them to keep talking. It's up to you to ask open-ended questions that keep the conversational ball rolling.

And it goes without saying that you've got to be genuinely interested in what the child has to say. You've got to want simply to listen, without throwing in judgments or spouting advice or cutting the child off to throw in your opinions.

Listening is the important thing. If the child knows you're basically interested in what he has to say, you won't have much trouble getting him or her to talk. My friend Bradley used to ask me for advice on how to talk to his absent children on the phone. "Just tell me what to say," he'd demand. "Give me a script." I tried to tell him he had the wrong attitude and that children see right through this sort of thing. They *know* if you're really interested and if you're really listening to what they say. If they don't get those vibes from you, they clam up.

I've had a lot of trouble myself with this, even though I haven't actually been a long-distance father and my phone calls to my son have only occurred during those two-week periods when he lives with his mother. It's so easy to start dominating the conversation myself, to fall into the role of the lecturing father or the answer man. Once I start doing that, however—boom! Communication is at an end. How can any child open up to a know-it-all?

So there are these two parts to talking to children long-distance: (1) you've got to be interested, and (2) you've got to really listen. If you just blab away and don't hear what the child is saying, your conversations will all be aborted before they start. For instance, if the child tells you he likes red cars, and you only say, "Oh, that's nice," the conversation will die. But if you lead him on with an interested question, like "What kind of cars?", you'll get a good conversation going. You may even get some surprises as he suddenly tells you, "Joey robbed a red car two nights ago and I went on a joyride with him. I don't have anybody else to tell it to, except you."

If they're worried or in trouble, the temptation to lecture or dictate will be strong. But resist it. The thing to do is simply to reassure them that it's okay to be upset and that the feeling will pass if they talk about it. To make this absolutely plain to them, you can occasionally let them see that *you* are upset or worried about things in *your* life. This is to let them know that other people have the same troubles they do. You can let them see the vulnerable you, the frightened you, or the discouraged you—as long as you don't get out of control and show them a desperate you. If they understand that you have feelings of confusion, disappointment, and loneliness just as they do, their love will flow back to give *you* support.

If you're trying to get a specific piece of information out of your child, don't come right out and demand it. Lead up to it obliquely. This applies especially to situations in which you suspect the child is in trouble or is having other difficulties and you're trying to discover what's wrong. The child may be reluctant to mention the matter or admit what's on his mind, and it will only make matters worse if you attack him with blunt questions. Ease into the conversation by an indirect route, then let the child himself broach the touchy subject. Thus, if you come right out and demand, "Are you flunking English?" he may say no or may hem and haw and not give you a straight answer. Whereas if you start out with a question that is only vaguely related to the problem, such as, "Is your English teacher any good?" you may get him talking on the subject to such an extent that *he* will then tell *you* that he's worried about possibly failing English.

It doesn't really matter what question you ask to get the ball rolling. Any one will do, as long as it introduces the general subject you want to talk about. Once started on this subject, the child will usually get around eventually to whatever is troubling him.

Interesting Ways to Keep in Touch

—Send postcards. Children love to receive things in the mail, especially pictures. Instead of writing one long letter every month, send a postcard or two every week. Even if you rarely travel outside your town or city, there are usually still quite a lot of postcards available at home. And a five-mile drive on Sunday to a neighboring town will provide a whole new supply. If you take plane or train trips, the airlines or railroads will often have postcards, too.

—Plan trips. If you see your children only during vacations or in the summer, you may often take trips with them. Planning the trip can provide a lot of contact between you during the months when you're separated. Discuss your itinerary and exchange suggestions by mail or phone. Send the children maps and tourist guides. You can often get lots of free literature from tourist offices in the states or cities you're going to visit. Give them your child's address and have the literature sent to him or her.

—Watch TV together. If your child has a favorite show, try watching it and then talking about it when you call next time. Or you can literally watch a show together by calling your child when it's on

TV. This can be very exciting in the case of a sports event or another special feature. If you and your child both love baseball, for instance, you can have a terrific time watching an inning of the World Series with the phone in your hand. (This costs money, of course, but if you call on Sunday, you can have fifteen or twenty minutes with your child pretty cheaply.)

—Know their teachers. If you can possibly arrange a trip to your children's town, by all means visit their school. Introduce yourself to their teachers. This will not only give you a valuable contact with a person close to your child but it will also provide you with a ready-made conversational subject when you telephone your child. If there are other important people in your child's life—a tennis coach, a Girl Scout leader, a music teacher—they can be even more valuable to you than schoolteachers.

—Play chess by mail. Not every child likes to play chess, and neither does every father, but if you and your child happen to share the interest, it's an ideal long-distance occupation. You each set up your own chessboard and then exchange your moves by mail or by phone. It can provide a running contact in your lives for weeks or months.

—Send snapshots. Children love to see pictures of you, your home, your friends, and the places you visit. A small camera is a good investment for that reason. Carry it with you everywhere, or keep it in the car. Then enclose a couple of pictures in all your letters. (By the way, write on the back of the picture the date and the subject. Twenty years later, someone will dig that snapshot out of a bottom drawer and be grateful to know what it portrays.)

—Receive papers and reports. Ask your children to send you copies of some of the work they do in school—papers, reports, drawings—anything at all that they are likely to be proud of. And then mention the work warmly in your next phone call.

—Try riddles or tongue-twisters. Most children love these things, just as they love jokes. They'll be perked up every time you call if you spring a riddle on them or tell them a new tongue-twister. The best way to have an endless supply is to go to your local library and put the problem into the hands of the librarian. He or she will usually be able to hunt up a book or magazine that has listings of hundreds of them.

—Send holiday cards. Instead of sending just a plain old letter every month, send a holiday card whenever you can. There are cards these days for more holidays than you imagined existed. Young children, especially, will get a kick out of funny cards for Groundhog Day, April Fools' Day, Halloween, and other holidays.

—Get distinctive stationery. Write your letters on red stationery, or round stationery, or bordered stationery. And send it in a matching envelope. It will catch the children's eyes. They'll look at the pile of mail in the mailbox and instantly know they have a letter from Dad.

—Send books. If your child likes to read (and not every child does), send him books on the subjects that interest him. These could be picture books, Nancy Drew mysteries, books about horses, computer manuals—anything at all that interests the child. Magazine subscriptions are okay, too, but the thrill of newness wears off after an issue or two. Books are a one-time proposition, and the child will be excited every time he receives one.

—Swap sports forecasts. If your child likes sports, you can trade "bets" on any and all games. (An actual money bet is even more exciting, if you approve of betting, and if you keep the amount small enough.) This is a very good way to keep yourself in the child's imagination, since all through the game, he or she will be thinking, "Who's going to win the bet—me or Dad?"

—Send clippings. This is an old tried-and-true way of keeping in touch. If you read newspapers or magazines, you'll always come across things that would be interesting to your child. Older children have special subjects that they're interested in; younger children always seem to like pictures of animals.

10.

FATHERS' ALMANAC

Problems
That Children Face at All Ages

There's a common knee-jerk reaction among single fathers: whenever the children have problems (especially emotional problems), Dad guiltily blames it on the separation. "If we hadn't split up, the children might not be having trouble now."

It's more common with newly separated men than with seasoned single parents, but the reaction is easy to hang on to and hard to get rid of completely, no matter how long you live alone with your children. There's always that little guilty voice whispering at the back of your mind that the children's adjustment problems at school . . . their puberty growing pains . . . their anger or their depression . . . can be traced one way or another back to the fact that they are children of divorce.

Of course this isn't true. Children in "normal" families have growing pains, too. It'll save a lot of wear and tear on your nerves if you realize that your children's emotional difficulties aren't all your fault. Some problems, it's true, are more common among children of divorced parents. On the assumption that it's a good idea to know in advance where the trouble spots tend to be, I want to provide this chapter on children's difficulties you should be prepared to face once you become a separated man.

How Separation Affects Children

There's no "best" time to get divorced. Children are always going to be affected by the separation. The best time to separate from your wife is when the two of you feel you can't stand to live with each other for another minute, regardless of what the children may feel about it. Children of different ages will be differently affected. Here, in a highly simplified way, are some of the typical reactions:

under age 3	They won't notice much.
ages 3–6	They'll be hurt.
ages 6–12	They'll tolerate it.
ages 12–18	They'll understand.

The worst time for divorce, from the children's point of view, is the three-to-six age period. They're likely to be more than just disgruntled or disappointed; they're likely to be really hurt. The two separating parents have to be more than usually understanding and supportive of children at this age. With preadolescents and teenagers, the separation doesn't hold so many dangers.

Infants (under one year)

Not many divorces take place when the child is still an actual infant, and when they do, the child usually remains with the mother. Shared custody is not often a good idea. As a result, the father won't, in most cases, find himself having to cope with the child's problems, and in any case, those problems are likely to be relatively straightforward ones of health and illness that affect all babies of that age.

The only advice for a father at this stage is to visit the child regularly (at the mother's). Keep your hand in, so to speak. You don't want the child to forget you. Not only that, but the baby needs to get a sense that there are other people in the world besides Mother. The best way for this to happen is if Dad puts in regular appearances.

Ages One to Three

Children in this age group, especially those under the age of two, may not miss you much when you move out (they'll be more affected if Mom moves out). Their awareness of the separation may be little more than a sense that you're not around as frequently as you used to be. They *will* be sensitive to your moods when you do visit them. You're liable to be nervous, overprotective, guilty, or simply ill at ease, especially if the separation is in its early days or your ex-wife hovers on the sidelines as you play with the child.

The child will pick up on these feelings of yours like a radar antenna, and there may be a reaction of tears, dislike, silence, or nervousness. Moral: try to be your "old self" when you see the child. This will do more good for him or her than anything else you can do.

At the age of two or thereabouts, however, things change. This is the age when the child begins to test his sense of self-identity by learning to say no.

"Pick up your toys, Danny."   "No."

"It's time for lunch, Susie."   "No."

"Do you want to go for a ride, Freddy?"   "No."

"Stop pulling the dog's tail, Marcia."   "No."

At this age, it may seem as if the child is forever refusing to cooperate, forever being negative, forever saying no. This is his way (a necessary and basically healthy way) of asserting himself and starting to gain a notion of what it means to be independent. So when you see the child and he says no to you, don't take it personally. Just let it roll off your back. At the same time, don't hesitate to put your foot down on occasion. The child's saying "No, no, no," is her way of testing the world and its limits, and so you have to give her a sense of *your* limits. Your wife is doing the same thing with the child, and it would give the child a warped view of adults if you were an absolute pushover and never opposed her when she said no.

There is one particular problem in separating when the child is two or three: the child may get the idea that he has driven the father away by being "bad" and always saying no. Dad can nip this problem in the bud quite easily by visiting frequently and regularly. The child will then see that he hasn't driven Dad away, and any neurotic guilt feelings will die before they grow too big.

And if the child is cranky or uncooperative during any particular visit, try not to leave without clearing up the bad feelings. Don't leave an opening for him to feel that he has driven you away. Let him know you'll definitely be back again.

Ages Three to Six

The danger age. These are the ages when separation is hardest on children. Children are no longer young enough to glide through the separation in a state of vagueness and incomprehension, but they are not yet old enough to grasp fully what is happening and to tolerate it. I remember when my wife and I split up, we brought our son, who was six years old at the time, into the living room and told him we had something to tell him. "I know," he said immediately, "you're splitting up." He had a friend whose parents had separated, and he had heard the phrase *splitting up* from him. He knew in general that splitting up was not a good thing, but he didn't know exactly what it was. This is typical of children this age: they grasp some of the situation, but not all.

They will be hurt and confused by the separation, and they won't know what to do about it. They will adjust—usually within a year or so—but they'll need a strong helping hand in the process. They are likely to react to the situation in one of several ways:

1. They'll ignore it. They refuse to credit what's happening, hoping that simply by closing their eyes, the situation will go away. They tend to think that if they don't actually admit to themselves what has happened, there'll be a chance that everything will go back to normal.

2. They'll regress to behavior they've outgrown. They talk baby talk, suck their thumbs, wet the bed.

3. They'll get hyperactive. They may always be on the go, always asking questions, always demanding attention, never stopping.

4. They'll cling to you a lot. They'll want constant attention. They may not want to let you out of their sight, and they may get upset if you talk to other people or even have a conversation on the telephone.

These forms of behavior will gradually dwindle away, but in the meantime, the children will need a lot of attention from you. They need contact and continuity. You've got to *be there* for them, and be there regularly. The more often you can see them, the better, but in any case, you should be steady in your visits. Canceling a visit at the last minute is guaranteed to upset them, and even being late to pick them up on Friday afternoon may give them a case of the jitters.

Much of their insecurity stems from fear of further loss. If they could put their fears into words, they might say, "If I don't grab Daddy and hold on to him, he may go away for good," or "When Daddy talks to somebody else, it means he doesn't like me," or "Since Daddy goes away, maybe Mommy is going to go away, too." (My own son periodically worried about my dying.)

Children will set great value on tokens of affection and approval. Words are best: "That's my girl." "I love you, too." "Did you really draw the picture all by yourself?" Phone calls are also good. Gifts and presents are okay, but large expensive ones are unnecessary. Here it's truly a case of It's the thought that counts. You certainly don't have to present them with armfuls of gifts every time you see them. They'll be happy enough to see *you*. And, of course, all children love to receive mail. At this age, they'll respond better to pictures than words. Send them postcards, pictures of horses ripped out of magazines, simple books, funny greeting cards, a poster with a crocodile on it . . . anything that you know will appeal to them.

HINT: Keep your letters, or the printed messages on your postcards, very short. Until your children can read, Mom will have to read your cards to them, and unless she is on the very best terms with you, she may tend to read them in sour or edgy tones.

The Oedipus stage. This is the period when children say things like, "I'm going to marry Daddy when I grow up," or "I'm going to marry Mommy." If the separation occurs when the children are in this stage, their reactions are as predictable as snow in winter.

Boys. The male child is hostile to Dad because Dad possesses Mom. He'd like to possess Mom himself. He often fantasizes getting rid of Dad somehow, even to the point of imagining Dad's death. When the separation occurs and Dad moves out, the child may think he actually *has* gotten rid of Dad. His reaction: guilt with a capital G. Fantasies are one thing, but when fantasies are seemingly turned into reality, it's more than he bargained for.

The surest way to let the Oedipal situation run its course without leaving a poisonous residue behind is to make sure the child sees you on a regular basis. He will then understand that he did not, and cannot, get rid of you—since here you are every Friday night.

He'll still have a normal amount of Oedipal hostility, of course, just as he would have if you and your wife were still together. This is nothing to worry about, and it calls for no extraordinary measures except to let his hostility (tantrums, anger, harsh words) roll off your back.

If it's your wife who moved out, the boy will think, "Dad got rid of Mom so I couldn't have her." He'll be furious with you, or depressed. Mom should visit regularly, so that it's obvious that she hasn't been driven away.

Girls. Girls at this stage want to possess Daddy, and they resent Mom for having him. If Dad leaves the household, her subconscious will say, "Mom knew I wanted Dad, and she drove him away so I couldn't have him." She may then develop some pretty harsh feelings toward Mom.

The best way to handle the problem, as with boys, is simply to see her regularly. If you're there every weekend, like clockwork, she'll understand that Mom did not, and cannot, get rid of you. In addition, reassure her that there's no competition between her and her mother: "I love you because you're very special. You're my daughter, and there's no one else in the whole world—not even Mommy—who can say that."

If it's your wife who moves out of the house, the girl may imagine that her fantasies of getting rid of Mom have actually succeeded. In that case, your wife should see the girl regularly so that she'll understand that Mom has not disappeared from the scene.

Ages Six to Ten

This is the age when children begin to see that there's a world outside the family. Children at this age can usually weather a separation better than younger children. They're not quite so family oriented and family dependent, so the split-up doesn't have to shake them as deeply. In addition, they are more sensitive to their parents' emotional state, which makes them a bit easier to handle: they're not quite so likely to throw tantrums at just the wrong moment . . . to demand attention just when you feel least able to give it . . . to cling to you like burrs just when you are ready to scream with frustration.

But, though they may tolerate the separation better than younger children, they don't really understand it much better, so they have many of the same reactions: (1) anger and rage, (2) silence and an urge to deny that the separation has occurred, (3) dependence on presents and other tokens of your affection, and (4) guilt.

Boys in the six-to-eight age range are particularly prone to bouts of anger if Dad has moved out. It's a way of covering their feeling of helplessness in the face of the separation. When they see you, they may "pay you back" for your "desertion" by indulging in disobedience and tantrums. And when they're with Mom, they may do exactly the same thing, since she's the only available target. There's no way to avoid their anger, but you won't be so bothered by it if you realize that it's "nothing personal" and just their way of protesting a situation they can't control. The best response is equanimity. As long as they're not actually being rude or breaking things, let them express their anger.

If you have more than one child, they may compete for your attention. This is a common reaction. In a two-parent household, the children can go to either Mommy or Daddy when they want attention. In a one-parent household, there's just *you*. It's bad enough if you only have one child, but it's worse if you have two or three. There's simply not enough parent time to go around. This tends to lead to quite a lot of scrapping among the children. Unfortunately, there's not much that can be done about this. There's no way you can satisfy each child's claims on your attention. The best compromise is simply to give each child as much attention as possible and, if they squabble among themselves, just let them do it. Opt out of their battles. Don't rush in to be the peacemaker every time you hear raised voices. As long as they're not physically hurting each other, let them settle the arguments themselves.

The six-to-ten years are the ones in which the children really begin to understand that there's a world outside the family. Their horizons expand. They go to school, they begin to have a peer group, they encounter authority figures besides their own parents. It's important that they have a secure base at home, so that they're free for "expanding." The more settled and amicable their home life, the better. If you have a bad relationship with your ex-wife, try not to let the kids get caught in the middle of it. Remember, their antennas are sensitive. They dread tension between their parents. If the parents fight, it's devastating to the children.

Children in this age group are likely to be particularly curious about your new life. Younger children care only about you, but the six-to-tens will be interested in your home, your work, your friends, what you eat, where you shop, and so on. It's part and parcel of their being more attuned to the outside world. And it's also a way to fix a concrete image of you in their minds, to nail you down, so to speak, so that it won't seem as though you're in danger of leaving the family again.

The six-to-tens are also likely to demand (even more than younger children) gifts and presents and other tokens of affection. Having lots of possessions is, for them, a compensation for not having more of you. You'll have to walk a delicate line between being a Dad-who-happens-to-give-presents and a present-giver-who-also-happens-to-be-Dad. Don't let the children turn you into a sort of mechanical Santa Claus, a person whose only identity is as a gift giver. The best way to do this is to avoid letting your gift giving fall into a routine. Provide gifts at odd intervals, so the children never know exactly when they're going to get something. And, since you don't have endless time to spend shopping and endless money to spend, keep things simple. If you spend too much money on stuff for the children, they'll inevitably get the impression that you're trying to buy their affection. My own experience with this problem is extensive, since I have a weakness for going overboard with the presents. My son once took me to task for it—he told me I was spending money as though I were rich and that it was time to cut down on the spending.

Children love to get things in the mail, so send plenty of letters if you're absent from them for periods longer than a couple of weeks.

Ages Ten to Twelve (Preteen)

This is the age when children really begin to congregate in peer groups. The sexes begin to mingle. It's a stormy age, and your children will usually have problems and growing pains even if you're not divorced.

This is also the running-away-from-home age. Children of divorced parents are more likely to run away than children in two-parent homes, simply because the single-parent children have a handy place to run to: the home of the other parent. Since it's usually Dad who is the "other" parent, the most common pattern is for children to run away from Mom's house and go to Dad's house.

This can be a tricky situation. In two-parent homes, children who run away usually return home very soon (in the vast majority of cases, as soon as it begins to get dark), because they don't know where to go. End of episode. In single-parent homes, the episode may not end so quickly and easily. If the child runs away from Mom's and goes to Dad's, there are then the questions: What is to be done with him or her? Should the child be returned promptly to Mom? Or should Dad harbor the runaway?

The guiding preference, as far as there is one, is this: except in dire situations, children at this age shouldn't be given a choice as to where they're going to live. If a young boy runs away and says, "I don't want to live with Mom, I want to live with Dad," he should usually not be allowed to do so. He shouldn't be the one to call the shots.

You'd be inhuman if you weren't flattered by a child wanting to come and live with you, but it's wrong to take him or her in with open arms, uncritically. It would be giving the child too much power, too much implicit approval. In running away, the child is trying to make a protest, but probably not that much of a protest. If you welcome him with open arms, you'll make it all the more difficult for him to go back to Mom if (as usually happens) he eventually wants to do so.

A thorough, unemotional discussion of the situation is the best thing, if you can manage it. Welcome the runaway, but also make him aware that he is (1) inconveniencing you by appearing on your doorstep without warning, (2) violating the terms of your family's custody agreement, (3) inconveniencing Mom by not telling her where he's going and what his plans are, and (4) taking the easy way out and avoiding, not confronting, his real feelings.

There is one thing that should not be said to a preteen: "If you don't like living with Mom, you can always come to live with me." It puts too much responsibility on the child when he or she isn't yet equipped to handle it.

The ten-to-twelves are especially likely to try to play it cool and cover their emotions if their parents separate during these years. They're the ones who act as though your separation is the most inconsequential thing in the world. Nevertheless, they are disturbed, under their blasé surfaces. Their concern comes out in a lot of questions about arrangements for the future. They have reached the age of rationality and they'll want to understand how, exactly, the separation will affect them: Will I be able to keep my dog? Who will drive me to baseball games? Who will cook Sunday dinner? What will my "official" address be? Will my friends still be able to visit me? Who will help me with my homework?

These questions are actually all variations on one deep-down underlying question: will there still be somebody to take care of me? Don't brush off their questions as trivial or meaningless. Answer them seriously. Or, if you get tired of doing that, answer the unspoken question by reassuring the child specifically that there will always be someone to take care of him and that he is not being left to fend for himself.

Preteens and teens usually begin to associate with and favor the parent of their own sex. They look for a model to imitate (as well as to surpass). Their egos start to be evident. (I remember my son standing in front of his mirror and asking me, "Dad, on a scale of one to ten, how would you rate my charisma?")

Because they tend to identify with one parent, they can't (as younger children do) live by the convenient "double standard" of being pro-Mom when they're with their mother and pro-Dad when they're with their father. Preteens may feel that they have to choose one parent over the other—anything else is "illogical." A certain amount of this is to be expected even in two-parent families, but in single-parent families, it can go too far. If a child begins thinking, "It's him against us," or "It's her against us," the stage is set for trouble.

To keep the situation from developing dangerously, you have to be patient and flexible. (Keep whispering the biblical words to yourself: all this shall pass.) A dash of compromise is often called for in your relationship with your children. Often a small change in custody or visiting arrangements will shake the relationship out of its accustomed ruts and initiate a sense of growth and change that will remove the child from his dangerous path. Consulting the child when making family decisions will help; so will explaining the reasons behind your decisions. Anything to avoid the appearance of being dictatorial and unwilling to listen.

Adolescents (Ages thirteen to nineteen)

At this age, children are semiadults and they can think for themselves. The problems you'll have with them are mostly the same problems married fathers have: arguments (they question your decisions and the reasons for them) and rebellion (they refuse outright to abide by your decisions). Aside from this, children in single-parent homes are likely to be especially independent, since they've had more responsibility and autonomy than other children. They will resent anything from you that smacks of dictatorial control. If you suddenly start making a lot of rules for their behavior (no sex—no drugs—be home by eleven, etc.), no matter how good your intentions are, they'll resent it.

Your relations with your teenagers will have to be based on compromise and mutual respect rather than on authority and control. Consult them about household rules, especially rules for their own behavior. Take their opinions and desires into account.

In particular, you'll have to be loose about when and how often they see you. They simply won't accept or tolerate the routinized, same-every-week arrangements that younger children thrive on. The most common problem is that they want to switch the dates of their next visit to you or don't want to visit you at all. "I've got a championship game and I've absolutely got to be there." "Marie's having a slumber party on Saturday and I'll die if I miss it." "I've got a test coming up and I'll flunk if I don't study."

The first rule is: be flexible. The second is: don't let them have their way *all* the time. If they have a realistic reason for wanting to switch dates on you or cancel their visit entirely, you'll probably have to accept it. At the same time, let them know that this is inconveniencing you and also disappointing you. Share your feelings about it, not to throw guilt on them but simply to let them know you're a feeling person.

It should be understood that they are to see you at more or less regular intervals, whether they like it or not. Within that framework, they should be allowed as much freedom as possible. If they don't want to see you ("Aw, Dad, it's so boring when we come to your place"), let them know that *you* need to see *them*. If they're right about it being boring, then ask them how to un-bore the visit —and listen to what they say. No matter how much they may complain about having constraints put on them, they need some limits. If you give in too easily to all their demands, you'll be surprised to see them eventually getting angry, itchy, and frustrated at not having a real parent.

When they're discontent, adolescents often threaten to move to the home of the other parent. Fathers who haven't seen their children for more than a weekend at a time since the separation may suddenly find that the children feel like leaving Mom and moving in with them. Or, if they have lived primarily with him, they may want to leave and go to Mom.

At this age, they must be listened to. If they express an interest or desire to move, it may actually be the best thing for them. They're old enough (unlike preteens) to handle the change and the responsibility inherent in it. If the question comes up, and you see that the child is serious about it, you'll have to negotiate. Listen to him, but don't allow any sudden or hasty decisions. If, for instance, your son wants to leave Mom's and move in with you, your position could be something like this: "You can come to me if all of us together decide it's the best thing. Let's stick with our current arrangement for two weeks and then see if you still feel the same way. If you do, then you can move in with me. But you must be fair to your mother."

Once the children reach the upper levels of adolescence (the age of seventeen or so), you'll have to accept their autonomy as adults or almost-adults. They've had enough independence and responsibility so that now they know their own minds and there's not much you can do to control or guide them. If they want to live with Mom—or with you—then that's what they want and there's no way to get around it.

If they announce that they want to go live with Mom, try not to take it personally and get all upset. They're not making a black-and-white choice of her over you. They have honest reasons for the choice. You'll simply have to listen to them and trust them. And keep reminding yourself of their love for you and yours for them.

Something like this happened to me one summer when my son chose to live with his mother, and I saw him only on weekends. He wanted to live with his mother because, although our homes were only five blocks apart, in his mother's neighborhood he was closer to his friends and felt safer. It was a reasonable reason, and I had to grit my teeth and go along with it. I learned to live with it because his happiness and peace of mind were my priorities. And I have to admit it worked out very well, as it usually does if everybody is honest and open.

11.

PUTTING IT ALL TOGETHER

Separation can hit a man in several different ways. Like a ton of bricks, coming down on you all at once with full intensity. Or it can be like a time-delay explosive, hoodwinking you with a period of deceptive normalcy before hitting you with the lethal whammy. Then again, it can come on like a distant depth charge, indistinct but ominous, then rocking you with a series of shocks that keep growing in intensity.

No matter what method it chooses, it does get you in the end. You can rarely avoid it. Sooner or later, you've got to go through a stretch of pretty rough water before you can reach calm seas again.

This is where experience counts. It's like those World War II movies about submarine crews. When the torpedo hit the sub, the new guy on the crew always lost his head, while the skipper just set his teeth and calmly issued an order for a damage report.

Unfortunately, when it comes to separation, most men are like the new guy on the crew. They haven't been through it before. They don't know what to expect. Not surprisingly, panic and confusion are likely to take over.

This is where it's really a lifesaver to have the help of other crew members who have been through it before. They're the ones who can tell you that just because the ship has been hit by a torpedo, that doesn't mean it's going to sink.

That, in a sense, is what I hope this book is—a way of getting through the crisis period with the help of guys who've been through it before.

I certainly know the sensation of being torpedoed by troubles so that there doesn't seem to be any possibility of remedying them all. I've never met a separated man who didn't have at least a tinge of that sensation. It seems to go with the territory. We all have to go through those weeks—or more likely months—of not being able to straighten out the messes we're in. And when the problems do finally begin to go away, it's not with a snap of the fingers; it's with one slow, miserable step after another.

So I feel that anything that can help get the ship back on course —or even give it a good stiff prod—is tremendously useful. Of course, neither this book nor any book can actually do the job for you. You can't just sit back and wait for the damage to repair itself. In the end, you've got to do it yourself. It's like having an operation for appendicitis—nobody can stand in for you. You're the one who's got to go under the knife.

But I think there is a strategy that will make things easier: start by attending to one problem, and then the rest of them will sort themselves out much more easily. It's like traffic gridlock in Manhattan: if even one lane of traffic were flowing, the gridlock could be broken up (slowly, to be sure, but it would work). It's only when there is no movement at all that things reach an impasse.

By the same token, I think movement is essential in life, too. When your separation has you feeling as if your life is gridlocked, then even the smallest trickle of movement can be a lifesaver. That's the most important thing—that first small bit of movement that shows there's life left in the old boy yet.

I think the practical translation of all this is: pick one area of your life and concentrate on it. For instance, if your children are uppermost in your mind, then you could turn to Chapter 3 of this book and work on some of the things it suggests for putting together a new life with your kids. Or, if you have a female friend who feels like the Right One to you, you might concentrate on that area of your life (see Chapter 6). And—here's the point—for the moment, ignore everything else. You can't do it all at once. Rome wasn't built in a day. Try not to even think about the rest of your life, or you may get too discouraged to take any action at all.

You might say it's like recovering from grief—say, the death of a loved one. For a while, you're simply shell-shocked, a basket case, unable to function. If you think about trying to get your life back to "normal," it simply seems like too big a job for any human being to undertake. The solution? *Don't* think about putting your life back together. Force everything out of your mind except for the one small thing, whatever it is, that you choose to focus your attention on. It could be food, it could be work, it could be your dog, it could be taking a long walk twice a day. This forceful focusing of your attention on a limited target gets you over the hump.

The same principle works when you're going through a separation. *Don't try to do everything at once.* The World War II submarine crew couldn't repair every flooded compartment at the same time. Neither can you. Take it one step at a time. Start with one particular thing you're relatively comfortable with, and go from there. This eventually will get the ship moving again. Once you've managed to make one small area of your life shipshape, the rest of your existence will be a lot easier to take care of.

If it's painful, well, that's life. Separation is just another pain that we have to go through. The American way often seems to be to try to deny the pain, or to give in to it too easily by allowing other people to coddle us in our misery. But there is no way out of it: you've got to live through your pain.

Even if you're feeling gloomy and hopeless, I hope this book has delivered two messages that can act as the light at the end of the tunnel:

One: You're not alone. We all go through it.

Two: It *will* get better. It doesn't last forever. You *will* work things out.

But I don't want to paint the picture too black. Usually it won't be this bad, and you won't have to take refuge in these reassurances.

You've got six areas of your life to work on: your children; your ex-wife; your home; your job; your female friends; and, last but not least, your self. You may start off working on only one of them—as I say, in the worst moments of your separation, you may not have the energy for anything else—but as you begin to be more of your old self, you'll eventually have to give attention to all six.

That's why I call this chapter Putting It All Together. Before your separation, these six elements of your life were put together in a specific arrangement that included marriage, wife, home, and so on. Now that you're separated, the Big Six have fallen apart and you have to build them up into a new structure that is right for your present existence as a single father. Your life during the separation period—and often for years afterward—is a set of variations on the theme of Putting It All Together.

Nobody—not I, not your friends, not the so-called experts—can tell you the right way to arrange those six main elements of your life. That is what *you* have to do. You can use the advice in this book as a guide, but once you've really started to patch up the various problems in your life, you don't need—or want—much more advice.

If being a single father does nothing else, it gives you a second chance in life. It gives you a chance to make a different life for yourself than you did the first time around. This is an extraordinary opportunity. Separation can be the kick in the pants that makes you into a different person—and, with any luck at all, a better one. After you've healed the wounds of your separation, you reemerge into the swing of things with a lot more to give and (cheers!) a lot more to get.

ON BEING FATHER

FRANK FERRARA

"I was on my own for the first time in my life; I was lonely; I missed having a family around me. I had to go through all the emotions I've since learned every separated man goes through: guilt, anger, loneliness, a sense of failure, insecurity, feelings of powerlessness and unfairness. My emotions were on a roller coaster. One day I'd be on top of the world with exhilaration at finally being free of all the marital obligations and expectations. The next day I'd be crying in my bed, unable to get up and face the day..." **—Frank Ferrara**

Frank Ferrara, the eldest of six children, was born and raised in Brooklyn. He joined the New York City Police Department at the age of twenty and has spent over seventeen years in various assignments from walking neighborhood beats to a moderator of a Sensitivity and Ethical Awareness Workshop. A gourmet chef who has aspirations of owning his own restaurant someday, Frank is also an avid athlete and has been a member and a coordinator of Single Father's Support Group for over five years. He lives in New York City with his son Christopher.

COVER PHOTOGRAPH © JANEART, LTD./IMAGE BANK
COVER DESIGN BY RICHARD ADELSON   0285
A DOUBLEDAY/DOLPHIN BOOK   ISBN: 0-385-19128-6